HOW TO MAKE HISTORIC
AMERICAN COSTUMES

FIGURE 1. Colonial Costumes, 1770

How to Make
HISTORIC
AMERICAN
COSTUMES

by

Mary Evans
and
William-Alan Landes

Illustrated by
Elizabeth Brooks
and
William-Alan Landes
Sophie Steel
C. W. Trout

PLAYERS PRESS, Inc.
P. O. Box 1132
Studio City, CA 91614-0132 U.S.A.

HOW TO MAKE HISTORIC AMERICAN COSTUMES
© Copyright, 1993, by William-Alan Landes
ISBN 0-88734-636-7
Library of Congress Catalog Number: 93-39731

PLAYERS PRESS, Inc.
P. O. Box 1132
Studio City, CA 91614-0132, U.S.A.

Library of Congress Cataloging-in-Publication Data

Evans, Mary, b. 1890.
    How to make historic American costumes / by Mary Evans and William-Alan
    Landes ; illustrated by Elizabeth Brooks ... [et. al.] -- Rev. and updated.
        p. cm.
    Previous ed. published 1976.
    Includes bibliographical references and index.
    ISBN 0-88734-636-7
    1. Costume design. 2. Costume--United States--History. I. Landes,
William-Alan. II. Brooks, Elizabeth. III. Title.
    TT507.E83 1994
    646.4'78--dc20   93-39731
                                             CIP

Simultaneously Published
U.S.A., U.K., Canada and Australia

Printed in the U.S.A.

Preface

Unless well versed in the art of cutting garments without a pattern, the maker of period or historic costumes can have a rather difficult time. Few books on historic costumes give any help on cutting and making of these garments. Commercial pattern makers, today, have several appropriate patterns. There are even costume houses that offer patterns which have been prepared especially for period accuracy. But usually these patterns are not easily available and rarely has this information reached the teacher, parent or local theatre company.

For the purpose of this book we have directed our approach to simplify the construction of Historic American costumes. The patterns shown have been worked out on the basis of two commercial or drafted patterns, or cut from actual garments: the simple shirtwaist for women's costumes and the pajama suit for those of men.

With the foundation or basic pattern of the correct size as a guide, the patterns for early American costumes may be readily developed. As a size sixteen pattern was used for developing the women's patterns and size thirty-eight chest for the men's, some variation in the measurements indicated in the diagrams will probably be needed for persons of different sizes. No seam allowances have been considered in the developments indicated, hence these must be allowed for when each individual garment is cut from cloth.

It is hoped that the task of the persons responsible for the costumes having an American historical background will be considerably lightened by this small book.

The authors gratefully acknowledge the many courtesies

that have been extended to them in the preparation of this material. Especial appreciation is rendered to the Museum of the American Indian, Heye Foundation, the Museum of the City of New York, the Museum of Natural History, Players U.S.A., and the Metropolitan Museum of Art for the privilege of studying authentic costumes in their collections.

Mary Evans
and
William-Alan Landes

Contents

Illustrations

ADDITIONAL ILLUSTRATIONS

COSTUMES OF
THE AMERICAN INDIANS

Figure 2. Iroquois Indians

1. INDIANS OF THE EASTERN WOODLANDS

Iroquois

The Indians with whom the early English, Dutch and other settlers came into contact when they reached the shores of the new land were those of the eastern woodland areas comprising what is now the country between eastern Canada and the Carolinas, the Atlantic Ocean and the valley of the Mississippi River. These Indians were agriculturists, chiefly, living in tepees and traveling the local waters in birchbark canoes. Their simple life required but little in the way of clothing. Wraps and loose garments were easily made from the skins of native animals, especially deer. They were decorated with designs wrought with the quills of the porcupine, with the hair of the moose, and with colorful beads. The skin garments were frequently stained

3

or painted with dyes of their own manufacture from roots, leaves and bark.

The Iroquois Indian, Figure 2, whose dress is selected as the most typical of the tribesmen of this area, was for the most part scantily clad in breech-cloth and moccasins. Some wore a brief skirt of doeskin reaching to the knees and held about the waist by a woven belt. To these basic garments he would add a tunic-like coat which extended to the knees and long deerskin leggings seamed up the front and elaborately decorated with beads.

Covering his straight black hair was a typical headdress consisting of a cap covered with short feathers. From the center of the crown sprung one or more eagle feathers. Some Indians preferred the roach made from the tails of deer and dyed red. Others shaved off their hair except for a narrow ridge extending over the top of the head from forehead to the back of the neck. The scalp lock hung from this.

The women of the forest area were also dressed in the light, supple skins of native deer. About the waist and hips and reaching below the knees was wrapped a deerskin skirt fringed along the edges and decorated with lace-like designs in beadwork. The simple upper body garment, likewise made of fringed deerskin, hung straight to the hips and fell over the arms in the form of sleeves.

The Iroquois woman wore knee-length leggings with the

seam worn directly in front, as did her men-folk, but her moccasins, of deerskin or moosehide, had the tongue sewed in as seen in Figure 2. Her long, straight black hair fell unconfined over her shoulders, or, at times, was braided in two braids bound with bits of gay red cloth. She wore neither feathers nor head covering of any kind. In especially cold weather she, like the men of the tribe, wrapped herself snugly in large skins from which the hair had not been removed. About her neck hung strings of wampum, or the teeth and claws of elk or bear.

In making costumes to represent those worn by the Indians of the forest regions, use fabric that will as nearly as possible resemble the texture of the soft deer and buckskins which those people used. If expense is not to be considered, skins of chamois are excellent. Cheaper materials are flannel, unbleached muslin, khaki and suede cloth dyed to simulate the color of the skins.

As far as possible select rather closely woven fabrics that do not ravel easily. And as the Indians threaded narrow thongs of leather through slashes in the garments, but little sewing is necessary to put together these costumes. If they are to be worn many times or in scenes depicting strenuous action, strips of adhesive tape may be pasted to the wrong side of the material where the slashes are to be made. Examples of this type of fastening are to be seen in the Iroquois tunics, Figure 2, and at the top of the woman's skirt, Figure 4.

To represent the Indian breech-cloth which was made of soft doeskin, cut a strip of muslin to measure from ten to eighteen inches in width and approximately forty-eight to sixty inches in length, depending on the size of the wearer. Place a narrow strip of muslin about the waist for a belt to support the breech-cloth.

To arrange the breech-cloth on the wearer, place one end of the strip of cloth next to the body in front and draw the end up under the belt. Let the end hang down almost to the knees. Place the other end of the cloth between the legs and under the belt at the back. The end in the back should be adjusted to the same length as that in front. When correctly adjusted, the breech-cloth forms short, smooth aprons across both front and back of the wearer.

The form of the man's tunic is shown in Figure 3. The sides and bottom should be cut into strips approximately three-eighths inch wide and four inches deep along the sides, and ten to twelve inches deep along the bottom to represent fringe. Through the slashes indicated at the side lace narrow strips of cloth to attach the front and back of the tunic. If preferred, they may be stitched together along the side.

The only sewing necessary in the making of this tunic is a bias facing about the neck line to prevent that edge stretching out of shape.

The woman's skirt and tunic, Figure 4, are also held on by lacing tape or narrow strips of fabric through the slashes. While the tunic was not fastened under the arm in any way, the front and back may be sewed together for a few inches above the

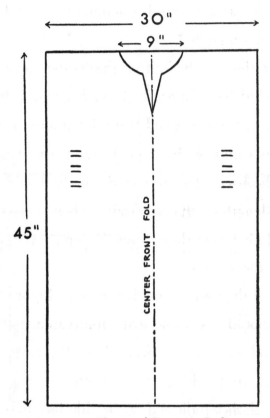

FIGURE 3. Tunic of Iroquois Indian

waist line. Both skirt and tunic should be fringed as shown in Figure 2.

The leggings of the eastern Indians were long for men, usually reaching nearly to the waist at the side. The leggings for the women were brief affairs extending from ankle to slightly above the knee.

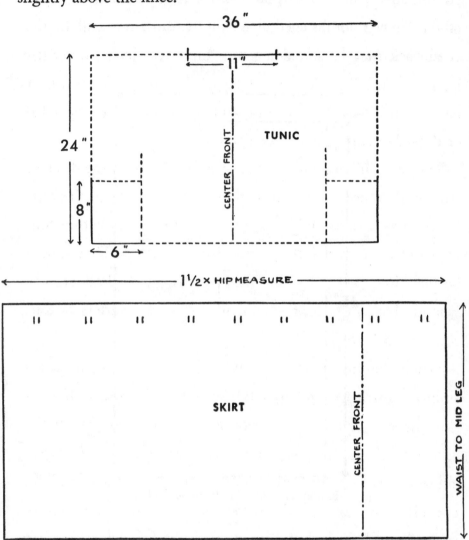

FIGURE 4. Tunic and Skirt of Iroquois Woman

For the men's leggings, cut two pieces of material, each approximately thirty inches long and twenty-three inches wide.

Fold lengthwise and stitch a seam to within four inches of the bottom edge. This seam is to be worn directly along the front of the leg. Curve the top edge slightly so that it will fit the crotch, then sew tapes at the seam and at the outer side of the legging. These should be tied to a belt around the waist. A decoration to simulate bead or quill work should be stenciled or drawn in crayon along the seam.

The woman's leggings should measure in length the distance from knee to heel; in width, slightly larger than the girth of the knee. They, too, should be seamed from the top to within four inches of the bottom and the seam worn in front. They should be held in place above the knee by strings of cloth or tape wound about the leg. The Indian squaw used garters of narrow woven bands.

When the Indian chose to wear a foot covering it was a simply constructed and usually elaborately decorated affair of skin shaped like a low slipper or a fairly high boot. While the varieties differed, they were in general based on two basic types, either a very soft moccasin made with upper and sole all in one piece, as worn by the woodland tribes, or the two-piece moccasin with the sole made of rawhide and the upper of a soft, tanned skin. This latter foot covering was commonly used by the Indians of the Plains area. The one-piece moccasin was of two main styles, as shown in the patterns, and in Figure 5 and Figure 6 following, the one with the center puckered seam prevailing among the Iroquois.

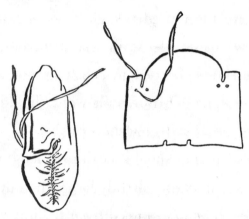

FIGURE 5. One-piece Indian Moccasin

For costume purposes, moccasins may be made of chamois skin, suede cloth or khaki. The bead decorations can be simulated by designs executed in crayon or paint.

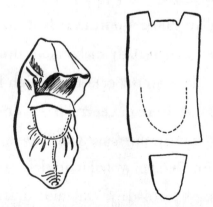

FIGURE 6. Indian Moccasin with Tongue

It is suggested that the patterns for the moccasin be made directly in unbleached muslin and fitted to the individual foot before being cut in actual fabric. It is wise to make moccasins for right and left feet. This may be done by placing the two right sides of the fabric together and cutting through the two thicknesses at the same time. Care should be taken before sewing to see that two moccasins are not made for the one foot.

In the patterns given here no seam allowances are included. If cloth is used, one-fourth inch seam should be allowed when cutting. If chamois is used no allowance is necessary, as a close but shallow overhanding stitch makes the most satisfactory joining for skins. The moccasins intended for performers taking very strenuous parts should not be fitted too tightly.

To make the one-piece moccasin illustrated in Figure 2 and Figure 5, draw the outline of the bare foot on the piece of muslin to be used as the pattern. Enclose this outline in a rectangle that measures two and one-fourth inches longer than the foot and nine and one-half inches wider than the measurement across the ball of the foot. Using the measurements given in Figure 7 make the pattern and cut along the dotted lines. Sew together the seams as indicated. The front seam should be pressed open, then gathered to fit the instep as shown in Figure 5. Under the turned back cuff cut or punch holes and draw through them the laces or tapes to be tied about the instep.

In Figure 2 the Iroquois woman is shown wearing the moccasin that is gathered to a tongue. This was another of the

soft-soled type of moccasin commonly worn by eastern tribesmen.

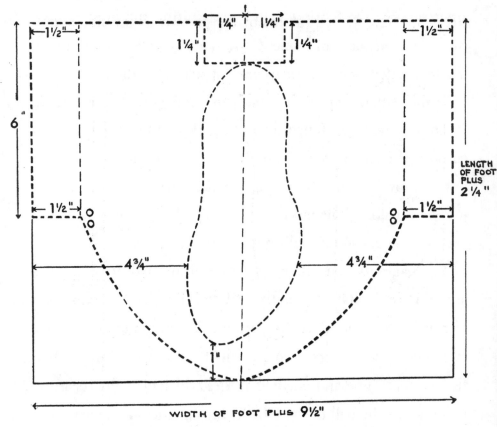

FIGURE 7. Pattern for One-piece Moccasin

Make the pattern for this moccasin by drawing the outline
of the bare foot on a piece of muslin. Draw around this outline a rectangle that is one and one-half inches longer than the
foot and two and one-half inches wider than the distance across
the ball of the foot. Follow the directions and measurements
indicated in Figure 8. Sew up the heel section first. Fold the

end of the rectangle near the toe of the foot in half and sew in a seam. Place the tip of the curve of the tongue at the end of this seam. Sew the side seams of the pattern to the side seams

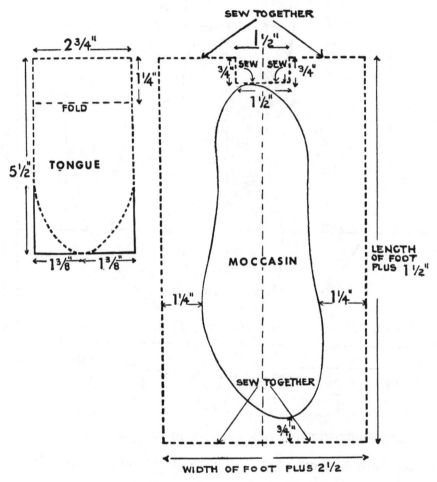

FIGURE 8. Pattern for Moccasin with Tongue

of the tongue as far as the fold of the flap on the tongue. Gather the fullness in the side sections to the tongue as shown in Figure 6.

The roach of the eastern Indian was made of deertails dyed red and sewed together. As decoration, three partially stripped feathers were attached to the tails so that they stood upright.

FIGURE 9. Indian Roach

To represent a roach, make a tight-fitting cap from the top of a stocking. Cut off the welt of the stocking and gather along the cut edge to form a *bowl-shaped* cap. Dye this the color of an Indian's skin, then sew to it through the center bunches of imitation hair in a two and one-half inch wide strip from forehead to neck. The hair can be made from hemp cord raveled and dyed red. Cut it into nine-inch lengths and sew the center of each bundle to the center of the cap so that they stand up in stiff bristles.

A narrow strip of long-haired black fur may be used instead

of this cap arrangement. Cut a strip of felt, or several thicknesses of cloth, into a long, narrow oval measuring ten inches by two inches. Sew the fur to this oval and hold it in place on the head by strings tied under the chin. Strip three turkey feathers, except for tufts at the tips, and sew them to the roach to give the effect shown in Figure 9.

The Iroquois feather hat was made of skin or cloth stretched over a framework of splints. To this were caught three overlapping circles of small feathers, the top and smallest circle being made of turkey marabou. At the center of the crown a large eagle feather swung in a socket so that it blew about in the wind.

For costume purposes the crown of an old felt hat, or the top of a stocking fitted to the wearer's head will serve satisfactorily. Sew three rows of small feathers to the foundation, starting with the lower and larger row. Attach one or more turkey feathers loosely to the center of the crown and surround it with a circle of turkey marabou. Bind the edge of the hat with a strip of cloth carrying designs to imitate quill or bead work.

The Iroquois and Eastern Woodland Indians were greatly affected by their contact with the Europeans. Although their style and color references did not change they soon preferred wool, cotton and broadcloth to animal skins.

FIGURE 10. Costumes of the Seminole Indians

Seminole

The Seminole Indians in Florida dress in a manner quite different from other Indians of North America. The cotton cloth of the white trader is worn by all members of the tribe regardless of sex. Colorful, voluminous and decorative, this costume is vibrant with very distinctive and bold geometric patterns in appliqué. A unique feature is the muffler-like arrangement of strings of beads about the neck and shoulders of the women.

Typical costumes for men and women are shown in Figure 10. They are simple to construct but require a great many yards of cloth. Unbleached muslin or inexpensive cottons with printed geometric designs will be satisfactory. The typical Indian designs can be stenciled or drawn on the cloth with colored crayons.

The man's costume is more intricate than that of the woman. A shirt of colored cotton cut to reach to the knees will serve for the undergarment. Stitch narrow colored tapes to the front to represent the designs on a typical garment. A strip of muslin approximately eight inches to ten inches in width and penciled or painted with geometric designs will serve as a broad belt while a small bandanna kerchief tied under the chin will finish the neck line.

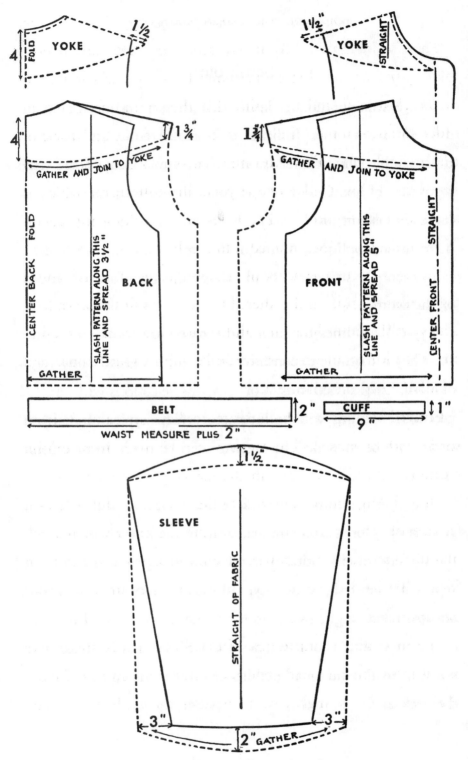

FIGURE II. Coat of Seminole Indian

The Seminole coat may be cut from the coat pattern of a man's pajamas suit. Figure 11 shows how the back and front of the pattern should be slashed lengthwise and separated in order to allow for the fullness in both the front and back of the Seminole coat. This extra material should be gathered and sewed to the lower edge of the yoke, the pattern for which is also shown in Figure 11. The lower edge of the waist section of the coat should be gathered into a belt.

The skirt section consists of straight pieces of fabric sewed together at the sides and gathered at the top to fit the waist belt. The skirt should be long enough to reach from waist to slightly above the knees. In width it should be approximately once and a half the hip measurement.

Fringed leggings and high-cut moccasins may be made from suede cloth or muslin. The leggings can be made from muslin pieces cut slightly larger than the leg measurement about the thigh and long enough to reach to the mid-leg. Fold each strip lengthwise, pin it about the leg to get the right fit, then stitch in a plain seam. Cut the lower edge into narrow strips to form fringe. To hold the legging in place use tapes to wind about the upper leg as a garter.

The moccasins characteristic of the Seminole's costume may be cut from the one-piece pattern described on page 11, Figure 5, allowing for the higher cut by making the ankle flap deeper.

The Seminole's head covering is turban-shaped and decorated with upstanding aigrets or feathers. A strip of material similar to that used for the coat may be wound about the head to form the hat shown in Figure 10.

The haircut of the Seminole Indian is decidedly unusual. A strip of hair about one inch wide is left across the front of the head between the temples. At right angles to this is a one-inch wide strip of hair extending across the top of the head from forehead to nape of neck where it is divided and braided into two hanging braids. Over each ear hangs a long black lock. The rest of the hair is cut close to the head.

When the turban is not worn in the costume play, this hair arrangement may be represented by sewing false hair, or bundles of dyed hemp cord, to a close-fitting skullcap made of muslin or a stocking top.

The woman's gown consists of a very full, ankle-length skirt, simple waist with long, full sleeves gathered into a cuff at the wrist, and a very deep bertha sewed to a deep yoke which fits the shoulders closely. Figure 12 indicates how the yoke may be cut from the foundation waist pattern.

The bertha itself is merely a strip of cloth about twelve or more inches in depth and in length once and a half or twice the measurement of the bottom of the entire yoke. After sewing up the shoulder seams of the yoke, gather the top of the bertha and stitch it to the bottom of the yoke. The neckline should be cut low enough to enable the wearer to slip the garment comfortably over her head. The yoke is frequently light in color and the bertha dark. If desired, a separate waist with long sleeves may be worn under the yoke and bertha, or sleeves may be sewed to the yoke itself.

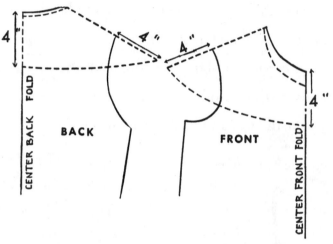

FIGURE 12. Yoke for Blouse of Seminole Woman

The skirt may be made of four widths of muslin seamed together and gathered at the top to a waistband. Bold designs should be stenciled or drawn on the skirt and edge of the bertha.

To the Seminole woman the innumerable strings of beads about her neck form the most important part of her costume. These may be simulated by cutting spaghetti into quarter-inch pieces, painting them in bright colors and forming strings in long lengths to be wound many, many times about the neck. Silver bracelets, earrings and finger rings as well as shining metal disks attached to the yoke will complete the woman's costume. The disks can be made of cardboard covered with tin foil or painted with silver radiator paint.

An enormous roll of hair, something like a halo, is worn across the woman's forehead and side of the head. To simulate this, comb the hair down over the face, pin a roll of cotton batting from ear to ear above the forehead, then comb the hair smoothly over this padding. Arrange the rest of the hair smoothly over the top and back of the head.

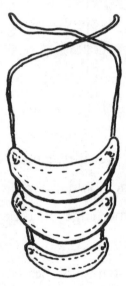

In addition to the unique muffler-like arrangement of beads, Seminoles used bracelets, beads, scalplocks and all types of silver adornments. Illustration 1 depicts three silver gorgets, as a necklace, connected with rawhide. The gorget appears as neckwear in many portraits of Seminole and Creek Chiefs such as Osceola, Creek Billy and even William Augustus Bowles.

ILLUSTRATION 1. Silver gorgets as neckwear.

2. INDIANS OF THE PLAINS

Dakotas and Blackfoot

The dress of the men belonging to the tribes known generally as the Plains Indians, of whom the Crow, Dakota, Cree and Blackfoot Indians are typical, was extremely simple, a breech-cloth and pair of moccasins comprising the two chief articles of wearing apparel. The entire skin of a buffalo, antelope or mountain sheep, or several skins of smaller animals pieced together served as a robe worn horizontally about the body in cold weather. Leggings and hard-soled moccasins protected the legs and feet from snakes, stones and other discomforts of the region.

On the dress occasions when it was worn, the shirt of the Plains Indian was a loose, straight-hanging garment reaching about to the thighs and wide enough to form a covering for

FIGURE 13. Costumes of the Dakota Indians

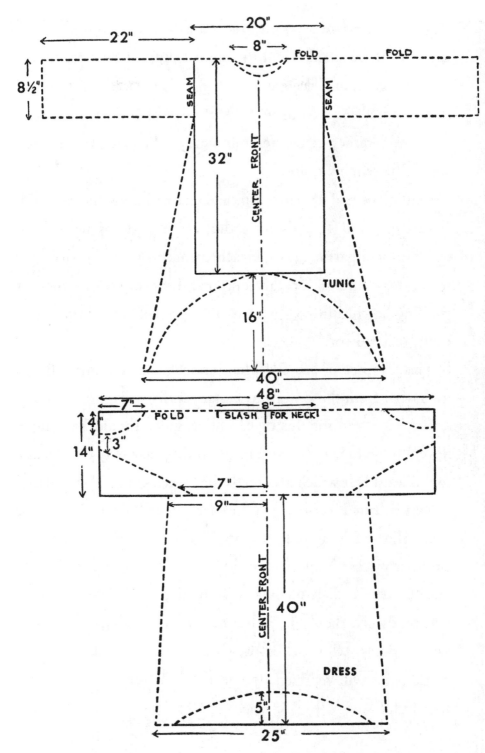

FIGURE 14. Tunic and Dress of the Dakota Indians

the arm. It was made from the tanned skins of deer, mountain sheep or goats and decorated with the claws, teeth and tails of small animals as well as with long wisps of human hair, with beads and rather elaborate embroidery executed in brilliantly colored porcupine quills.

Figures 13 and 18 show typical shirts of Plains Indians with Figures 14 and 19 indicating the simple patterns needed for cutting these garments. Unbleached muslin or suede cloth are satisfactory fabrics for this purpose. Use colored crayons or running stitches in coarse yarns to represent the trimming of quills or beadwork.

The leggings of the Blackfoot and Dakota Indians differed somewhat from those worn by eastern Indians. Figure 15 shows a simple pattern for this type. The leggings should have tapes sewed to the top, at side and front, so that they may be attached to the waist belt which also holds the breech-cloth. The material should be fitted to the leg and either stitched along the side or small slits made as indicated in Figure 15. Narrow strips of cloth, or pieces of tape, passed through these and tied will simulate the true Indian method of fastening the leggings. Fringe and beadwork should be indicated for the leggings of the Dakota Indians, while strips of white rabbit's fur spotted with black paint will represent the ermine tails used by the Blackfoot Indians.

The two-piece, or hard-soled moccasin is the characteristic foot covering of the Plains Indians. They used a soft tanned skin, heavily decorated, for the upper and a rawhide for the sole. Figure 16 shows a pattern for the hard-soled moccasin. Buckram would be excellent for the sole, and muslin for the

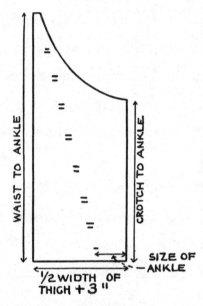

FIGURE 15. Typical Leggings of the Plains Indians

upper. Place the bare foot on a piece of buckram and draw the outline of the foot, A. Make a pattern for the upper as shown in B. Cut on the dotted lines, allowing narrow seams, and sew up the back seam first. With close overhanding stitches sew the upper, B, to the sole, A. Punch holes as indicated and draw through tapes or laces to hold the moccasin about the ankle.

A center part in the hair from forehead to the nape of the

neck and a long braid hanging over each shoulder was the cus-
tomary hair arrangement of the Plains Indian. Strips of colored
cloth were frequently braided with the hair or the braid was

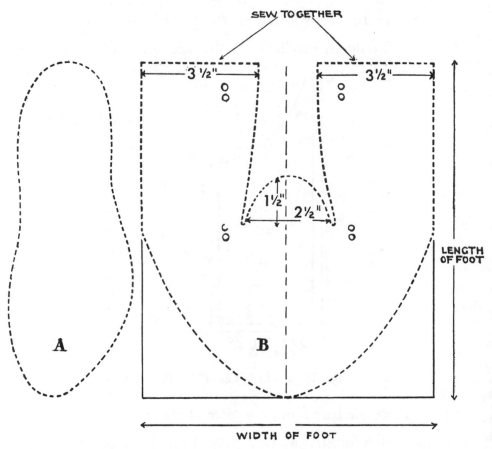

FIGURE 16. Pattern for Hard-soled Moccasin

wrapped with bands of soft leather enriched with beaded designs.

To represent the long, black hair of the Indian it will be necessary to make a wig from black horsehair or ordinary wrapping

twine dyed black. First make a close-fitting cap from black sateen or cambric. This should cover the head from forehead to nape of neck. Indicate with white crayon the center part from forehead to neck. Cut the cord into strands measuring

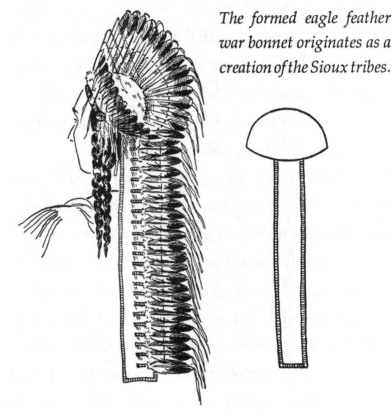

The formed eagle feather war bonnet originates as a creation of the Sioux tribes.

FIGURE 17. Indian War Bonnet

about fifty inches in length. Lay the centers of the strands along the part line and sew securely in place to the foundation cap. Two additional rows of stitching about two inches apart on each side of the center will be needed to hold the strands in position on the foundation. Braid the loose strands over each ear into long braids. Wrap the braids with narrow strips of colored cloth.

Eagle feathers worn in the hair were significant of prowess on the part of the wearer. The privilege of wearing the feather war bonnet, Figure 17, with the long tail of many eagle feathers was reserved for the few of really distinguished accomplishments. Ordinarily the Plains Indian, man as well as woman, wore no head covering, though a few tribes in the north would don caps of fur in extremely cold weather.

The making of the war bonnet is a task which requires patience as well as many feathers. Fifty or more white turkey or goose feathers with the tips dyed dark brown may be used in place of eagle feathers. Tiny chicken feathers or turkey marabou will be needed to attach to the quill of each of the larger feathers. The crown of an old felt hat and about one-eighth of a yard of red flannel, strips of white rabbit fur to represent ermine, several yards of gay ribbon or narrow strips of red cloth, and strands of hemp rope dyed red to imitate hair complete the list of needed equipment.

First, fit the felt crown to the head, so that it comes down on the forehead. Place two or three marabou feathers at the quill end of each large feather and bind them securely in place with red yarn or narrow strips of red cloth. Sew thirty of the large feathers to the edge of the felt crown, Figure 17, placing the largest feathers across the front. With a small awl, punch a hole sidewise in the shaft of each feather about five inches from the end of the quill and through it pass a very heavy thread or a fine cord. This is for the purpose of supporting the feathers securely in position. Leave a space of one inch or more between adjoining feathers and knot the thread about each shaft before proceeding to the next feather.

To make the tail piece, first bind with ribbon the edges of a strip of red flannel eight inches wide and long enough to reach to the wearer's heels, or for a shorter tail piece, to the wearer's hip.

Each of the twenty or more feathers for the tail piece must be so prepared for attaching that the feathers will stand at right angles to the flannel. With a sharp knife, and starting about one inch above the end of the quill, cut away, diagonally, part of the quill. Bend the pointed end back on the quill and wrap several times with a strong thread, at the same time binding in a small marabou. This provides a loop at the end of the feather.

Through the lengthwise center of the tail piece cut pairs of one-half inch long slashes about one-fourth inch apart, and with approximately three-fourths of an inch between each group of slits. The slits must be cut at right angles to the center line. Place a needle threaded with a long, heavy thread through from the under side of the last slit at the bottom of the tail, pass it through the looped end of one feather, then down through the second of the first pair of slits. From there proceed to the second pair and repeat the operation of attaching the remaining feathers to the tail piece.

In order to hold the entire long strip of feathers at right angles to the tail, sew them all together in a long line as you did the feathers around the crown of the bonnet. Punch holes sidewise through the shaft of each feather about three or four inches from the wrapped end.

Sew the tail piece to the back of the bonnet as in Figure 17. Finish the edge of the bonnet with a one-inch band of cloth decorated with crayons to represent a beaded band. Sew or paste tiny feathers on the crown section in three overlapping rows, with the smallest circle at the very center of the crown of marabou. To the tip of each of the large feathers paste a few strands of cord or heavy thread. These are to represent scalp locks. Sew the "plume," a long feather stripped of all but the very tip feathers, at the exact center of the bonnet's crown.

Hard-soled moccasins, short, bead-trimmed leggings reaching slightly above the knee where they were held by garters, and a one-piece garment extending from shoulder to ankle formed the usual costume of the woman of the Crow, Dakota, Blackfoot, Arapaho and a few other tribes of the Plains. Two entire elkskins made the back and front of the garment with extra pieces sewn to form an upper section that was part yoke, part cape, richly decorated with bead ornamentation. Closed at the shoulder and at both sides from waist to the bottom of the skirt, this garment was usually fringed along the bottom, the sides and along the edges of the cape-like upper section. As the natural contour of the skins was preserved the dress was much shorter in the front and back than at the sides. About the waist was worn by women of the Dakotas a broad belt of leather ornamented with and fastened by large disks of silver. Sioux women, however, preferred broad belts with colorful patterns worked in beads. In addition to fringe and beads, long, narrow strips of skins were threaded through slashes on the surface of the elkskin and formed tassel-like, all-over trimming.

Like the men of the tribe, the Indian woman of the northern plains wrapped herself in winter in a large buffalo skin robe. Her hair was usually worn in two long braids over the shoulders, older women preferring to let theirs hang free and unconfined.

Figure 14 shows the pattern for the dress of the Dakota Indian woman, and Figure 19 the pattern for that of the Blackfoot Indian woman. Heavy quality unbleached muslin makes satisfactory material for these dresses. The edges of the garments should be slashed to represent fringe. Boldly worked designs in

FIGURE 18. Costumes of the Blackfoot Indians

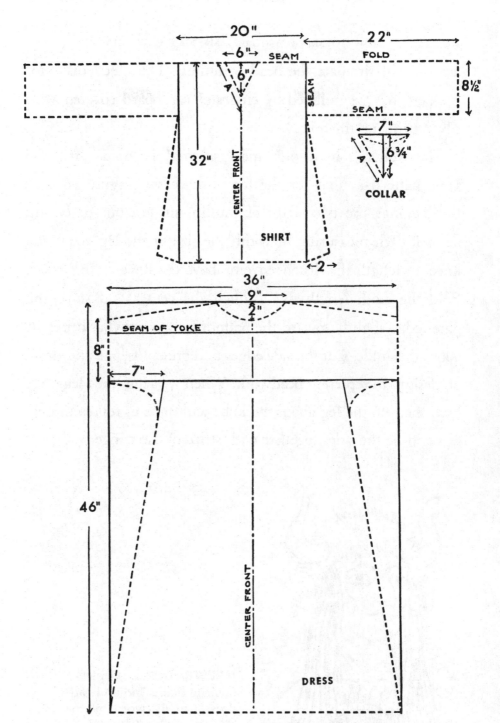

FIGURE 19. Shirt and Dress of the Blackfoot Indians

crayon will simulate the bead trimming. The metal disks for the belt may be imitated by circles of cardboard covered with silver paint or tin foil.

The woman's hard-soled moccasin may be made after the same pattern as that for the man's moccasin, Figure 16. For the leggings use two strips of muslin, suede cloth or outing flannel, each measuring in width the size of the leg above the knee, in length the distance from above the knee to the ankle. Fold the cloth lengthwise through the center and slope the outer edge slightly toward the bottom for a somewhat better fit about the ankle. Cut the side edges to represent fringe and draw on designs to represent beadwork. When wearing these leggings bind them to the leg about the knee with tape to represent garters and tie the sides together with strips of the fringe.

ILLUSTRATION 2. Depicts a favorite Plains Indian head-dress usually worn by the "Medicine Man." Its style of buffalo horns and buffalo hide varied only in the hide used. The Blackfoot preferred ermine skins.

3. INDIANS OF THE SOUTHWEST

Navaho

The Navaho Indians of today residing in the open country of western New Mexico and northeastern Arizona, in general use cloth rather than skins for their costumes and are extremely fond of wearing black and dark blue.

In Figure 20 is illustrated the typical dress of the Navaho man and woman. The man's costume may be developed from the pattern of a pajamas coat and trousers fitting the latter rather closely and leaving the side seam unstitched for five inches above the hem line. Any inexpensive fabric in tan, blue or black may be used.

In making the shirt from the coat pattern cut the center front and back along the fold of the cloth. As some Navaho men wear their shirts outside the trousers the shirt

FIGURE 20. Costumes of the Navaho Indians

should be cut to reach to the knees. Cut the V-shaped neckline large enough for the shirt to be slipped on over the head. In order to show the heavy silver bracelets cut the sleeves two inches shorter than the pattern.

String together large wooden beads of varied colors for the necklace, and for the silver disks on the belt paint circles of cardboard, cut three inches in diameter, with silver radiator paint. If a more gleaming texture is desired sew or attach with wire the tops of jelly glasses or smoothly cut tops of tin cans to two thicknesses of muslin folded to a width of three inches for the belt itself.

The Navaho man's hair is long, knotted up in back as shown in Figure 20 and bound with strips of colored cloth. A wig may be made as described on page 28 and arranged in this manner. A length of red cloth or a bandanna may be tied about the head as illustrated.

The Navaho woman wears a simple, long-sleeved blouse fastened in the front with silver buttons. Her full skirt, reaching to the ankles, is of dark wool fabric. No pattern is needed for the skirt as it may be made from three or four straight lengths of brown or blue muslin stitched together and gathered at the top to fit a waistband. The blouse may be cut from a foundation pattern as shown in Figure 21.

Jewelry made by native craftsmen is worn by every Navaho

woman in great abundance. Her wrists, fingers and neck are encircled with silver ornaments studded with turquoise. Her earrings are as elaborate as those worn by her husband but the disks on her belt are not usually as heavy and large as are those

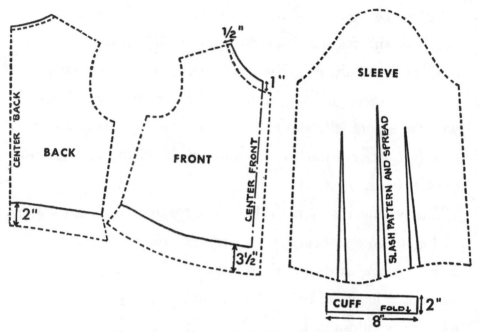

FIGURE 21. Blouse of the Navaho Woman

on his broad belt. Silver costume jewelry similar to the true Navaho jewelry is easy to obtain and should be worn if possible.

The woman's long hair is looped up at the nape of the neck and bound with colored strips after the fashion of the men's hair dressing. If a wig should be necessary to represent this hair arrangement follow the directions for making a wig as given on page 28.

As hard-soled moccasins are worn by Navaho women as well as by men the same pattern can be used for both. See page 28, Figure 16. To the top of the moccasin attach a long strip of cloth about one and a half inches wide and wrap this about the leg in the form of a puttee.

Colorful and patterned hand-woven blankets serve as wraps for the men and women of the Navaho tribes. These are placed over the shoulders, wrapped around the body and held in front with both hands. If true Navaho blankets cannot be borrowed for stage use sew together two strips of gray or tan muslin to form a blanket measuring fifty inches by sixty inches or larger, according to the size of the wearer. Stencil or paint on the geometric designs typical of these blankets.

Hopi

While the breech-cloth is the only article of wearing apparel of some of the Hopi Indians of northeastern Arizona many are clad in long, close-fitting trousers and straight-hanging fringed shirts of skins. The latter garments may be cut from four rectangular pieces of muslin, cambric or khaki as illustrated in Figure 23. Narrow strips of cloth cut into the form of fringe may be sewed to the front of the shirt in the V shape shown in Figure 22. The trousers may be cut from a pajamas pattern and,

FIGURE 22. Costumes of Hopi Indians

as in the case of the trousers of the Navaho, the side seam should be left open for five inches above the hem line.

Hopi Indians, in general, wear a high-cut moccasin, one that reaches two inches above the ankle. To represent this type follow the pattern on page 13, Figure 8, adding a two-inch-wide cuff to the top of the moccasin.

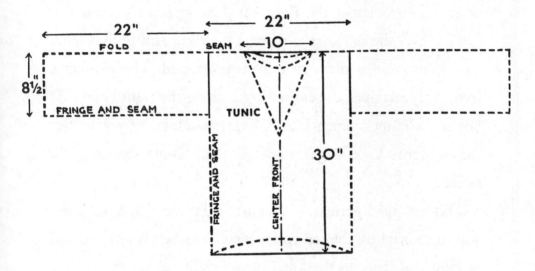

FIGURE 23. Hopi Tunic

To represent the shoulder-length hair cut of the Hopi man follow the directions for making a wig on page 28 and cut the strands of string or artificial hair to reach almost to the shoulder. Bind a strip of colored cloth about the forehead.

The dress of the Hopi woman, shown in Figure 22, is extremely easy to represent as it is in actuality a blanket-type gown of dark wool, frequently blue, with colored stripes forming a border along one end, woven on a primitive loom. It reaches from shoulder to below the knee and is somewhat larger in width than the measurement of the hips. It is folded in two lengthwise and so placed about the body that the lengthwise fold is at the wearer's left side, under the arm. The front and back are laced or sewed together at the right shoulder to form a seam that extends over the shoulder and down the right arm to the elbow. The left shoulder and arm remain uncovered. The blanket is frequently left open the entire length along the right hand side, but some Hopi women lace it together rather loosely so that the straight, knee-length undergarment shows between the lacings.

This wrapped garment is caught at the waist by a long belt woven in brightly colored native wool. The belt is long enough to loop and hang to the knee on the right side of the wearer. For costume purposes this belt may be made by stitching together colored tapes or strips of cloth cut one inch in width and ninety inches in length. The strips may be left unstitched for several inches at each end to imitate fringe.

Many strings of turquoise or silver beads with silver moon-shaped pendants adorn the neck of the Hopi woman, while heavy silver bracelets and earrings add further decorative notes. Men also wear heavy earrings of silver.

Attached to the top of the woman's moccasin is a long strip of leather which is wound about the leg from the ankle to above the knee.

Married women wear their hair in a long braid, but unmarried women have a very decorative hair arrangement consisting

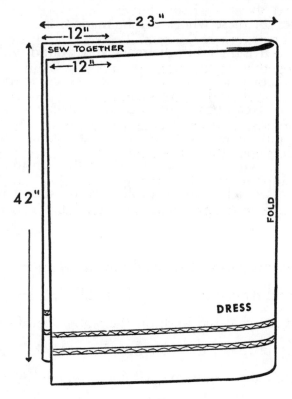

FIGURE 24. Dress of the Hopi Woman

of a huge roll over each ear. This is considered symbolic of the squash blossom. First the hair is parted from forehead to neck, then a heavy wire shaped like a croquet wicket, U, and about six inches in length, is placed close to the girl's head just above one ear. The long black hair is wound in and out of this wire prong in a figure 8 motion until the prong is covered. The ends of the hair are then wrapped round and round between the head and the prong and tied in place. A similarly formed whorl is arranged over the other ear.

Substitutes for these whorls can be made from circles of cardboard four to five inches in diameter and wound with strips of black cambric or black yarn. Cut a one-inch circle in the center of each piece of cardboard and pad the cardboard with cotton before wrapping it with the cambric or the yarn. Part the hair from forehead to neck then wind and pin the hair in a knot over each ear. Pin securely a padded roll to each knot of hair.

COSTUMES OF THE ESKIMOS

FIGURE 25. Costumes of the Eskimos

4. COSTUMES OF THE ESKIMOS

While the cut of the garments worn by the Eskimos varies in the different regions between Alaska and Greenland the number of garments and the materials from which they are fashioned are alike for all. The skins of native seal and reindeer are cut and sewed into warm, protective shirts, tunics, trousers and high boots. Occasionally denim or jean brought in by traders is utilized by the Hudson Bay Eskimo for his trousers. The garments are practically alike for both men and women but the tunics of the Eskimo women at Point Barrow and in the Hudson Bay region have lance-shaped tails both back and front. Women's high boots frequently reach to the waist while the men's boots extend to the knee. The only head covering is a hood which is usually attached to the neck of the blouse.

As can be seen in Figure 26 the pattern for the tunic of the Eskimo is based on three rectangles. The measurements given in the diagram should be varied somewhat according to the size of the wearer of the garment. The neckline should be cut large enough for the tunic to be put on over the head and should have attached to it the one-piece hood shown in Figure 25. The pattern for the hood, worn by the Eskimo of Labrador, is the same as that used for the costume of the Eskimo woman shown on page 52.

The trousers worn by men and women are practically alike and may be cut from a full pajamas pattern, the woman's being a trifle longer than the man's trousers. For the high boots use the pattern for the one-piece Indian moccasin with a tongue, Figure 8, page 13. To the top of the moccasin sew a strip of cloth long enough to reach almost to the knee and large enough at the top to fit over the trousers. Place the seam directly in the front shaping it to fit rather loosely about the ankle. Hold the boot in place below the knee by a two-inch-wide strip of cloth twisted into a soft rope and tied at the front.

The tunic of the Eskimo woman is rather close-fitting about the waist and is cut with a long, apron-like tab in the back and a somewhat shorter one in front. A hood of generous proportions is attached to the neckline of the tunic. In Figure 25, which illustrates the dress of the women in the region around Hudson Bay, the hood is shown falling back over the woman's shoulders. Figure 27 shows the adaptation of a foundation waist

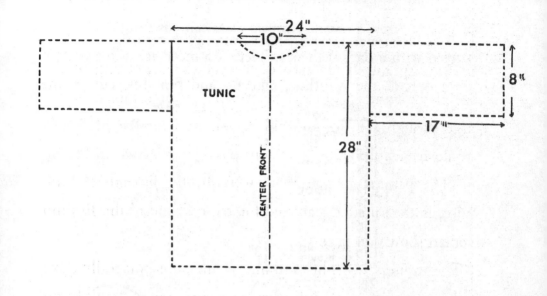

TUNIC

24"

10"

8"

17"

28"

CENTER FRONT

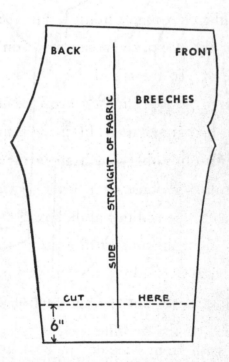

BACK   FRONT

BREECHES

STRAIGHT OF FABRIC

SIDE

CUT   HERE

6"

FIGURE 26. Tunic and Breeches of the Eskimo Man

pattern with a dart at the shoulder. If a more accessible pattern has a dart at the waistline, take up and pin this dart in the

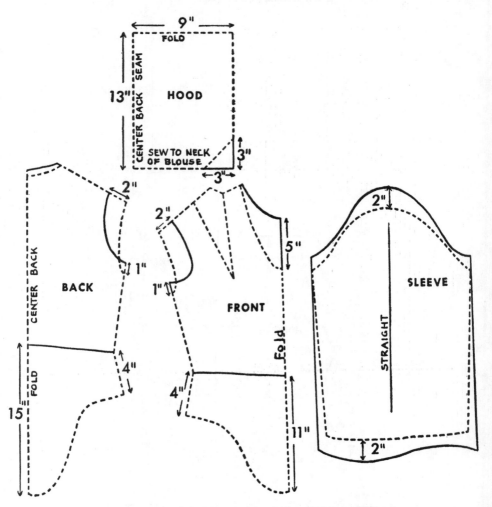

FIGURE 27. Bodice and Hood of the Eskimo Woman

pattern then slash from shoulder to bust line spreading the pattern at that point. The dart will now be from the shoulder in the actual garment.

To represent the seal and reindeer skins which the Eskimos use for their warm garments the maker of costumes should use a napped fabric such as Canton flannel or suede cloth, if possible, in a brown or tan color. The dark lines on the tunic of the woman represent strips of dark fur inset in the lighter fur of the tunic itself. On the flannel tunic these lines may be indicated with tape or dark brown crayon. Tunic, trousers and boots should be made of the same fabrics.

ILLUSTRATION 3. Eskimo in a waterproof version of the tunic (parka). Leather or seal skin boots, fur inside.

ILLUSTRATION 4. Canadian Eskimo from Bafflin Islands. Boots and mittens of seal skin fur, turned inside. Fringed tunic (parka) and short trousers of caribou hide.

COSTUMES OF THE COLONISTS

FIGURE 28. Costumes of the Colonists of Virginia

5. THE VIRGINIANS

Many of the English men and women who settled in Virginia, Maryland and the Carolinas were, on the whole, people of wealth. Their plantations in the new country soon provided them with the comfortable surroundings to which they were accustomed in England. Among the good things of life which they possessed and enjoyed were the clothes cut according to the fashion prevailing in England and on the Continent. Nearly every ship brought them handsome fabrics and trimmings as well as new garments and authentic news of the latest cut in doublets and petticoats. The short doublets which the men wore when they departed from the England of James I were later supplanted by the long coats and waistcoats of the court dress of Charles II.

The doublet and breeches of the Virginian during the first quarter of the sixteenth century are illustrated in Figure 28.

A pattern for the waist-length doublet may be cut from the coat pattern of a pajama suit as shown in Figure 29. In order to obtain a close fit for the doublet pin the coat pattern together at the shoulders and hold it to the person for whom the doublet

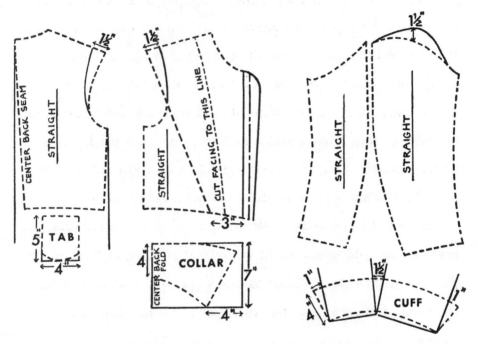

FIGURE 29. Doublet of the Virginian Colonist

is to be made. See that the center lines of the pattern are in the correct position on the person. Pin in a lengthwise tuck, both front and back of the coat through the shoulder seam. This alteration will shorten the shoulder length and give a closer fitting garment. Indicate the waistline and pin in a new under-arm seam. Use this fitted pattern as the basic pattern for the front and back of the doublet and the measurements given in Figure 29.

For the two-piece, close sleeve use a commercial pattern or one cut from a man's sack coat. For the hanging sleeve use a piece of fabric twenty-four inches long and seven inches wide. Pin this to the top of the sleeve before sewing the latter to the armscye of the doublet. For the epaulet arrangement use loops of tape or strips of cloth cut one and a quarter inches wide.

The tabs about the waistline should be made from the same material as the doublet and attached to it. Two thicknesses of fabric stitched along three sides and turned right side out will give the necessary body to these important decorations.

For the crisp collar use a stiff material such as white organdie. Place a wire along the outer edge of the collar to be sure the desired shape will be obtained and kept. If a ruff is desired as the neck finish follow the directions for making a ruff on page 62.

The breeches may be made from the trousers of a pajama pattern. See Figure 30. Cut the breeches well below the knee and gather the end of each leg section into bands that fit the knees tightly. Tie a ribbon or tape over the knee band. Golf stockings should be worn with these breeches if the suit is supposed to be of wool. Silk stockings should be worn if the suit is of velvet.

As the Virginia planters used rich fabrics for their doublets and breeches, materials should be used that will simulate handsome velvets, cloth and brocade as closely as possible. Unbleached muslin dyed somewhat irregularly will give the effect

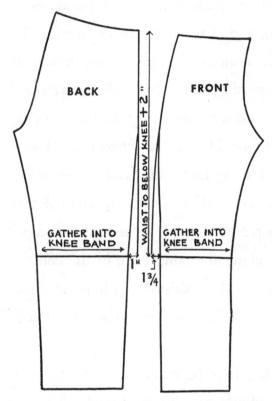

FIGURE 30. Breeches of the Virginian Colonist

of the lights and shadows of velvet. Inexpensive drapery material will substitute for brocade, outing flannel for velvet.

A man's large-brimmed hat will serve satisfactorily for the Virginian's hat. Place a ribbon or a piece of upholsterer's braid around the crown and an ostrich feather at the left side. If no such feather is obtainable make a substitute one from tissue paper.

For the woman's close-fitting and pointed bodice develop a pattern from a basic waist pattern as shown in Figure 31.

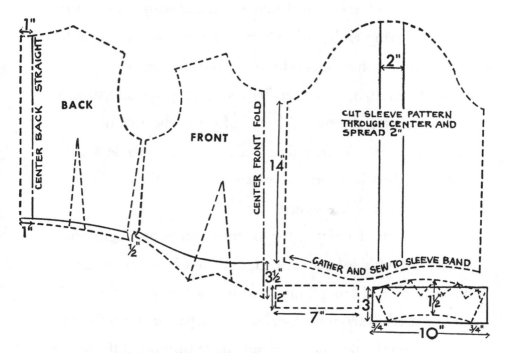

FIGURE 31. Bodice and Sleeve for Costume of the Virginian Colonist

Fasten it down the center front under one of the braids or tapes stitched on the waist for decoration, or down the center back. Looped tapes sewed into the armscye will give the epaulet effect seen in Figure 28.

In order to obtain the *barrel-shaped silhouette* so fashionable in those days it may be necessary to make and wear a padded roll about the hips. To construct this type of farthingale cut a strip of muslin five inches longer than the waist measure and eleven inches in width. Fold the strip lengthwise and stitch the long seam. Stuff the tube thus formed with cotton until a sausage-like roll is obtained. Close each end with a strong thread or cord leaving ends with which to tie the ends of the roll together after it has been adjusted about the person.

White tarlatan, paper cambric or inexpensive lace should be satisfactory for the turned back cuffs and the ruff of the Virginian colonist. At that time ruffs were formidable affairs of stiffly starched linen or lace extending five or more inches beyond the neck of the wearer.

Cut a strip of tarlatan five or more yards in length and six inches in width. Along each edge stitch a hem three-eighths of an inch wide. Through one hem pass a fine wire, through the other a needle carrying a long, narrow tape. Draw up the length of fabric on the tape to a size suitable to tie around the wearer's neck. Shape the wired edge of the ruff into figures of 8 and crease the cloth into folds until the desired fluted effect is obtained. When the ruff has been adjusted to the neck pin together the outer edges of the ruff where they meet.

Tarlatan, inexpensive lace or net should be used for the cap whose pattern is indicated in Figure 32. Whip a very fine wire to the outer edge or thread the wire in and out of the tarlatan as near the cut edge as possible. Pin the cap to the wearer's hair and bend the wire so that the center point comes down over the forehead, like the Mary Stuart cap, and the sides stand in wing form above the temples.

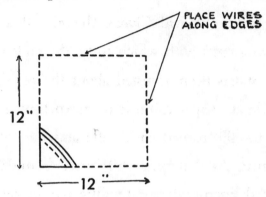

FIGURE 32. Cap for Woman of the Virginian Colony

Gauntlet gloves and circular-shaped cloaks were worn by both sexes. To make the cape stitch together two pieces of muslin each measuring forty-five inches in length, and fold lengthwise along the stitched seam. From one corner measure three inches along this fold. From the same corner measure three inches along the adjoining side. Draw a curved line between these points and cut on that line for the neckline of the cape. Cut and curve the bottom edge of the material in a line parallel to the neckline curve. Bind the neckline with tape, leaving ends of tape to tie under the ruff. Men wore a short, circular cape jauntily draped over one shoulder.

FIGURE 33. Costumes of the Colonists of the Carolinas

6. THE CAROLINIANS

The Englishmen who established settlements in the Carolinas in the year 1670 and those who came later with their women-folk brought with them many of the comforts and luxuries to which they were accustomed during the time of the Common-wealth or at the court of Charles II. Their clothes were elaborate in cut and decoration, reflecting the mode of the time. Fine broadcloth, serge, plush, camlet, a mixture consisting of wool and silk, and linen were found in many of the masculine cos-tumes. Brocade, velvet, satin and flowered silks were favorites with the women. Woolens, cottons and linens were utilized for everyday garments and for those of lowly station in life. Buttons of silver, pewter, brass and mohair fastened the long coats and waistcoats of the men, while handmade lace was worn by men as well as women.

There are available many inexpensive fabrics which may be

used as substitutes for the rich fabrics of the seventeenth century. Sateen, rayon satin and brocade of very inexpensive quality will make up well for the women's gowns; Canton flannel, khaki and unbleached muslin dyed in the desired colors will serve for the plush and broadcloth of the fashionable southern gentlemen.

Buttons of cardboard painted with gold, bronze or silver radiator paint make acceptable fastenings for the long coat and waistcoat. Pieces of soutache or other narrow braid may be pasted or sewed beside the slits used for buttonholes. In some cases the buttonholes may be indicated with India ink or gilt paint. The slits for the buttonholes should be reinforced with adhesive tape between the coat and the coat facing.

The long coat and full breeches worn by the master of a Carolina plantation are illustrated in Figure 33, and the method of developing the pattern for the coat is shown in Figure 34. The pattern for the long waistcoat, similar to that worn by the Quaker, Figure 46, may be adapted from that cut from a man's modern vest. For the full breeches use the same trouser pattern suggested for the breeches of the Virginian colonist, Figure 30, cutting them both fuller and longer about the knees. In order to save time and labor, stitch a three-quarter-inch hem at the bottom of each breeches leg and insert elastic in the hems. This will insure a close fit at the knee.

For the puff sleeves showing below the three-quarter length sleeve of the man's coat, use a piece of white cambric or lawn fifteen inches by twenty inches. Sew up the side seam, then

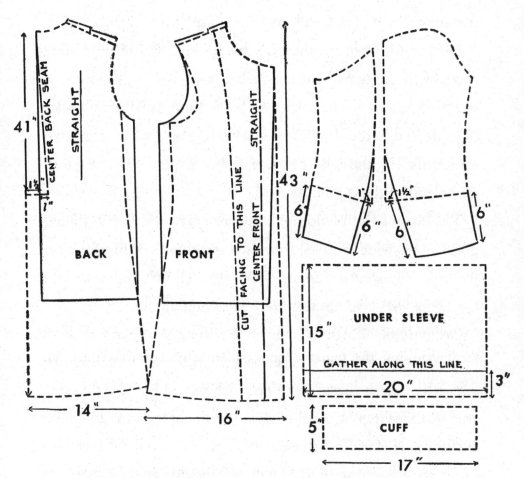

FIGURE 34. Coat of the Carolina Colonist

along one end stitch a half-inch hem and insert in it a narrow elastic. At the other end make a very narrow hem. One and one-half inches above this hem place several rows of running stitches and draw up the fullness to fit the wrist rather loosely. If desired, a narrow tuck may be used in place of the gathering and a narrow, round elastic passed through the tuck. This detachable sleeve puff will take the place of a full shirt sleeve.

For the cravat about the neck use a long strip of fine white cheesecloth or lawn about five inches wide and long enough to wrap twice around the throat, to be tied in a small bow under the chin and fall to the wearer's chest. Inexpensive lace, tarlatan scalloped along the edges or strips of shelf paper should be sewed to the end of the cravat.

The broad ribbon holding the sword may be of heavy ribbon, three inches wide or made from two thicknesses of muslin with painted or crayoned design. Upholsterer's gilt braid sewed to the edges will give a somewhat richer appearance.

Ordinary black ties will answer for shoes. Make a tongue of black felt or heavy black paper backed with buckram, sew it to a length of black elastic about one inch in width and fasten this around the instep of the shoe. Place at the base of the tongue a buckle made of cardboard painted silver or covered with tin foil. Long stockings of wool, cotton or silk should be worn with this costume.

Whenever possible, wigs should be rented from a costumer. A substitute headdress can be made by sewing strips of crepe hair or crepe paper to a foundation made from the top of a stocking. Cut off the welt from a stocking and gather up the cut edge so that the top fits the head closely. Cut black, brown or tan crepe paper into strips one inch wide and about twenty inches long. Roll up the strips tightly, paste or sew the free ends to the foundation cap, unroll the strips and twist them into curls. Cut and sew on as many strips as necessary to give the effect of abundant, shoulder-length curls. Work from the edge of the foundation cap up toward the center so that the points of attachment are covered.

The man's hat should be large in brim and have one plume on the side. The pattern for the Puritan's hat, page 77, can be easily modified by cutting the brim a trifle wider, by making the crown lower and by using tarlatan rather than buckram for the foundation of the crown. Dent the crown to give a soft, draped effect. Canton flannel may be used for the hat covering.

The bodice worn by the women of the Carolinas during the late seventeenth century was close-fitting and pointed at the front of the waistline. For dress occasions the neckline was low over the shoulders as well as front and back. The exquisite lace of the period edged both neckline and the elbow-length puffed sleeves of white that emerged from the cap-like sleeves of the bodice. Petticoats were of elaborate materials and richly trimmed at the hem line with lace. The skirt of the dress itself was open in front, and, to display the decorative underskirt even better,

was draped at the hips and held by bows of ribbon. In the back
it was long enough to form a slight train. Feather fans, long
white gloves, a short string of pearls, and silk slippers completed the evening costume of every lady, while her hair was
softly curled about her face and hung in one or more long curls
over the shoulder.

Figure 35 shows how to adapt the foundation waist and
sleeve patterns to give the effects shown in Figure 33. The puff
sleeves may be made in the same manner as the man's shirt
sleeve, page 67, with elastic at the top and bottom to hold them
securely on the arm, or they may be cut from the sleeve pattern shown in Figure 35. Loops of ribbon or tape, or a narrow
ruffle of self-fabric should be used to edge the short sleeve of
the bodice.

To give the desired effect, it may be necessary to line the
front of the bodice with a stiff fabric such as tarlatan or canvas.
Bows of ribbon, tape or narrow fabric should be sewed to the
center front of the bodice. The bodice should fasten in the back.

Strips of tarlatan, about three inches wide, can be cut to
imitate fairly heavy lace for petticoat, neck and sleeves. If gold
or silver lace or gimp is desired, either paint or spray the tarlatan
with radiator paint.

The underskirt may be made of three or more widths of
glazed plain chintz to simulate satin, while for the dress skirt,

of the same fabric as the bodice, Canton flannel, sateen or inexpensive rayon drapery fabric will give the desired textural effect. The overskirt should be cut from straight lengths of cloth eight

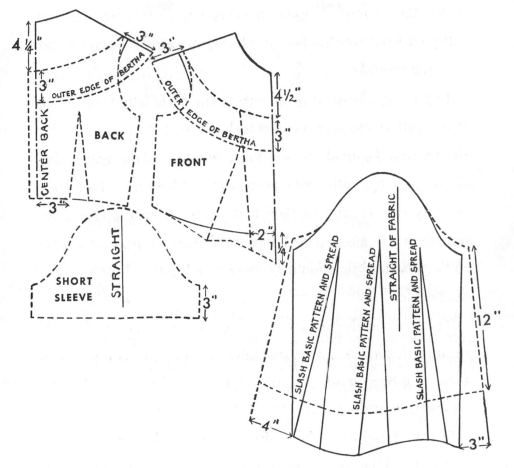

FIGURE 35. Bodice, Sleeves and Bertha of Costume for Woman of the Carolinas

to ten inches longer than the petticoat, sewed to a waistband or to the bodice, if desired, but left open in front. Loop it up on each side, either pin or sew in place and add the bows of ribbon.

For the fan, cut an oval of cardboard for a framework and to each side of the foundation paste larger ovals of crepe paper cut into fine fringe around the edges. Cut several smaller ovals, fringe the edges and paste them through the center to the foundation with rubber cement. Both sides of the frame should be covered in this way. Cut two strips of cardboard to the shape desired for the handle and attach them with wire to the fan. Paint the handles with enamel or lacquer.

Dress the hair softly and if necessary use false curls long enough to hang well over the shoulder.

When selecting fabrics, remember that men wore elaborate brocades as well as women and that abundant curls, ribbons and other adornments were found in men's hair, even more so than women.

Additional women's patterns and construction information can be found in PERIOD COSTUMES FOR STAGE AND SCREEN 1500-1800 by Jean Hunnisett. Men's patterns and detail can be found in MEN'S COSTUME, CUT AND FASHION OF THE 17th AND 18th CENTURY by R. I. Davis.

7. THE PURITANS

The early settlers of our New England states arrived in the new country clothed in the fashions prevailing in England during the reign of Charles I, and while they strongly disapproved of many of the religious, social and political practices of the homeland, they continued to be interested in its dress. In fact, the majority of them for many years ordered the wardrobes of the entire family from England. The Pilgrims and Puritans were, however, much averse to elaborate, extravagant dress and prohibited the wearing of the then fashionable ribbons, laces and feathers as well as costly fabrics.

While tanned deerskins were frequently used for the doublets and breeches of many a hardworking Puritan, plain but good-wearing cloth of wool and linen in rich, warm russet, brown, green and purple were the commonly used fabrics for the costume of the Puritan man and his spouse. Holland linen, snowy-

FIGURE 36. Costumes of the Puritans

white and untrimmed, formed the falling band and turned
back cuffs for both. While hooks and eyes very generally re-

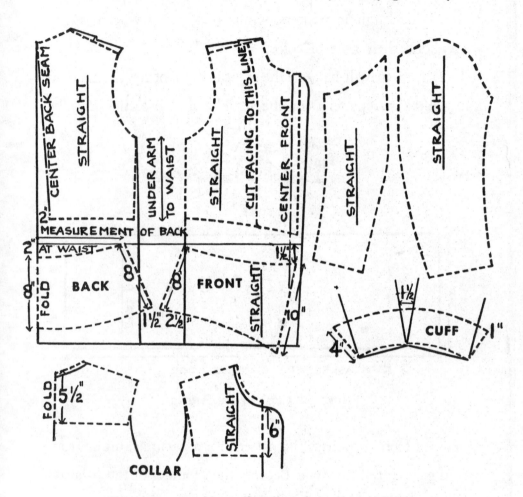

FIGURE 37. Doublet and Collar of the Puritan Man

placed silver and pewter buttons, the latter are much in evidence
in portraits of the early Puritan fathers and are listed in their
inventories and wills. A silver buckle held the ribbon at the

base of the tall-crowned felt hat. Voluminous cloaks, warmly lined, enveloped the wearer and protected him from the chills of the New England winters, while long, green woolen stockings added their note of color.

In Figure 36 will be seen the typical dress of a Puritan man and woman. A pattern for the doublet and breeches may be

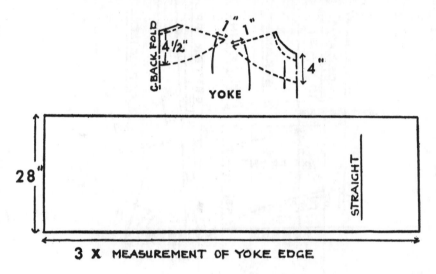

FIGURE 38. Cloak of the Puritan

developed from a commercial pattern for a pajamas suit or from an old garment of this type. Because the shoulder of the pajamas coat is rather long and the coat is fairly loose fitting, it would be wise to pin a lengthwise tuck in both back and front of the pattern through the shoulder. Hold the pattern to the person who is to wear the garment and pin up the tuck until the desired fit is obtained. It will be necessary to add to the top of the sleeve pattern the amount taken from the length of the shoulder. The adjusted pattern may then be used as the basic pattern for the doublet as shown in Figure 37. Doublets at that time were slightly short-waisted. Care should be taken to cut the peplum long enough to be placed at a slightly raised waistline.

Drilling, or muslin dyed in rich, dark tones, or in black are heavy enough in texture for doublet, breeches and cape. Cambric

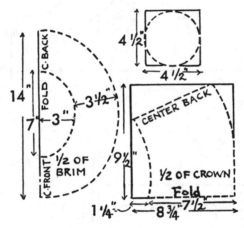

FIGURE 39. Hat of the Puritan

or bleached muslin make up well for the collars and cuffs. If time permits these should be made double and slightly starched.

For the full breeches of the Puritan, adapt a pajamas pattern as illustrated in Figure 30. Lap the front of the side seam over the back and hold in place with buttons. Gather the bottom of the breeches into a one-inch band that fits closely below the knee and tie with a ribbon.

A simple pattern for a Puritan cape is to be found in Figure 38, the yoke for the cape being developed from the front

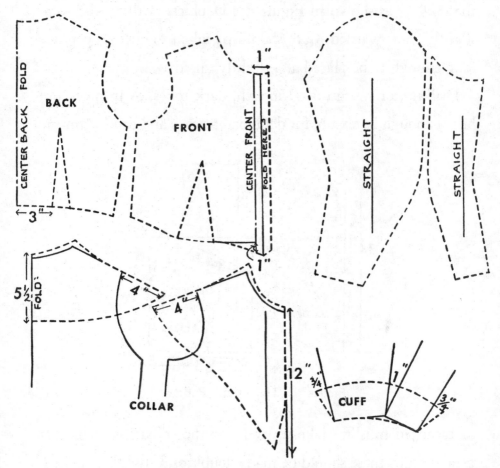

FIGURE 40. Costume of Puritan Woman

and back of a pajamas coat pattern. The cape should be made of a fairly heavy cloth, drilling or flannelette, and lined.

Buckram and black flannelette or suede cloth are needed for the tall-crowned Puritan hat. Follow the directions in Figure

39, modifying as necessary to meet the measurements for the wearer's head size. When a satisfactory pattern has been made, cut tip, brim and crown from buckram, sew up the center back seams and sew this tip to the top of the crown. Cut the brim from two thicknesses of the flannelette and with these cover the brim of buckram. Cover the sloping crown and the tip with

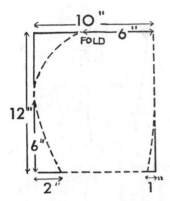

FIGURE 41. Cap of Puritan and Quaker Woman

the flannelette and then attach the crown to the brim. Wrap a one-inch wide ribbon around the base of the crown and at the center front slip the ends of the ribbon through a buckle cut from cardboard and painted with silver paint. A similar but larger buckle is necessary to hold a two-inch belt of imitation leather.

The pointed, fitted bodice of the Puritan woman is readily made from a basic waist pattern darted in both front and back to achieve the close, smooth fit about the waist. See Figure 40.

Full petticoats can be made from straight lengths of cambric or muslin stitched together and gathered into waistbands. For the draped up skirt, leave one seam of a straight-cut skirt open for the front, drape up the skirt on the sides and in the back, tacking it in place to the underskirt. Cut a length of white muslin for the apron, and gather the top into a belt.

FIGURE 42. Cape of Puritan Woman

The collar and cuffs should be cut from the patterns made as indicated in Figure 37 and, like those of the men, made of cambric or heavy lawn. Two or more sets of tapes should be sewed to the front edges of the collar and tied together in neat bows.

The woman's bonnet may be made from a dark colored muslin with a turned back section of white cambric or lawn cut separately and basted to the front edge of the bonnet. Figure 41 illustrates the simple pattern needed for the bonnet. Modify the pattern as necessary to fit the wearer. The bonnet should be fastened by tapes or ribbons tied under the chin.

The Puritan woman's cape, Figure 42, was very similar to that worn by the Puritan men, and frequently was red in color. Cut four pieces of muslin measuring in length from shoulder tip to ankle. Stitch the four pieces together, leaving the fourth seam open. Gather the top of this large rectangle and attach it to the yoke which has been cut from the back and front of a basic waist pattern, Figure 38. Use a muslin heavy enough to fall in the folds characteristic of heavy wool cloth.

ILLUSTRATION 5. A stylish Puritan (Pilgrim) in less extreme dress. A dark circular cloth cloak with a lining of silk. Dark red cassock, grey breeches and buff leather boots and gloves. Feathers in his hat and a walking stick to finish. (For pattern and details see MEN'S COSTUME, CUT AND FASHION OF THE 17th AND 18th CENTURY.) Many Puritans took a more cavalier approach to their clothes.

FIGURE 43. Costumes of the Dutch Colonists

8. THE DUTCH

The Dutch Colonists who landed on these shores and founded New Amsterdam in 1623 were thrifty people who wore sturdy woolens and linens when intent on their daily affairs but who, nevertheless, enjoyed very fine dress on gala occasions. The costumes so delightfully depicted by the Dutch masters of the seventeenth century found their counterpart in the dress of the Dutch patroon and his lady of the Manhattan Colony. Handsome velvets, silks, fine linens, laces and furs were plentiful with none of the restrictions of the New England Colonists to prohibit and limit their use. Jewelry was abundant; buttons and buckles of gold set with precious gems fastened the garments of men as well as of women. Color was found in the dress of all. Purple, blue, red and yellow were frequently mentioned in old records of the period. The Dutch housewife was skilled in the art of using native barks for coloring her ample petticoats, full samares and generous aprons.

In Figure 43 may be seen the simple, everyday dress of the Dutch settler. For gala events he would wear a doublet with slashed sleeves showing the white linen shirt beneath, a falling ruff edged with lace and ribbons at his instep as well as broad sashes about his knees. His breeches would be of velvet or cloth of fine texture.

It is suggested that for the doublet and breeches shown on page 82 the same patterns made for the Puritan man's doublet and breeches be used for costume purposes, but that the breeches be cut with much greater fullness. The collar and cuff pattern is identical with that used for the Puritan dress. The crown of the hat should be much lower than that in the Puritan's hat and one or more plumes should be placed along the edge of the brim. A woman's large felt hat would be satisfactory.

Some Dutch men wore their hair short, others as shown in Figure 43. If a wig cannot be obtained from a costumer one can be made of fine yarn sewed to a close-fitting foundation cap of muslin.

The skirts of the Dutch woman's costume must be very full, at least five yards around the bottom, and several in number. Heavy muslin should be acceptable for the petticoats, and sateen for the dress skirt. The top petticoat should be strong in color so that when the dress skirt is lifted the brightness of the petticoat will add to the color scheme of the entire costume. The working woman tucked up her dress skirt in front and caught it high in the back. Figure 44.

A close-fitting bodice with sleeves of three-quarter length and a turned down collar, or a kerchief, should acompany the

The Dutch women wore much the same styles for work. The primary difference was in the quality of the fabrics used. They were frugal people but prided themselves on quality; they used the finest cloth and linen to trim their plain garments, made of the best fabrics available or their own homespun. Dutch women were known for their business and investment skills as well as their impeccably managed and decorated homes.

FIGURE 44. Dutch Woman Dressed for Work

full skirts if the jacket or samare shown in Figure 43, is not worn. This was a loose-fitting garment of velvet, brocade or satin edged all around with a band of fur. Figure 45 shows how the pattern for the samare is constructed. To represent the fur border sew thick strips of cotton batting along the edge of the jacket and sleeves.

The cap of the Dutch woman was similar to that worn by

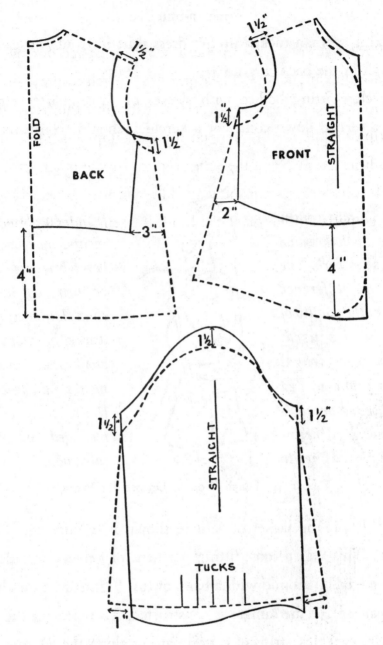

FIGURE 45. Samare of Dutch Woman

the Puritan woman. The pattern shown on page 79 may be used for the caps of both. The cap for the Dutch costume should be lined and cut deep enough to turn back over the front edge. A strip of white cambric pinned across the top of the head will be sufficient to indicate the inner cap unless the outer covering is to be removed during the play. The hair should be arranged in large puffs at the side of the head, the remainder knotted at the top.

ILLUSTRATION 6. A Dutch working man of about 1650. Note that except for the collar, cuff and hat basically the same costume as the man in Figure 43 can be used. The fabric is probably homespun and not as fine for work clothes.

FIGURE 46. Costumes of the Quakers

9. THE QUAKERS

A comparison of the costumes worn by all men of standing in the various parts of the Colonies and that of the Quakers of Philadelphia during the latter part of the seventeenth century reveals that the Quaker, man as well as woman, followed the fashions of the day, eliminating only the "superfluities." King Charles II and William Penn both were clad in a full-skirted coat, waistcoat reaching almost to the knee and breeches of the same generous proportions. The Quaker, however, used much restraint in the choice of trimmings. The ruffles of his shirt sleeves and his cravat were devoid of lace, his large brimmed hat of plumes, and his coat buttons the glitter of gems. In the eighteenth century the costume of the Quaker followed the cutaway lines of the fashionable velvet coats and the close fit of the satin knee breeches. But the fabrics were unpretentious and the colors limited to brown and gray.

For the Quaker costume coat, waistcoat and breeches may all be cut from the patterns used for the same garments of the gentleman from Carolina. Figure 34 shows how the coat may be adapted from the pajamas suit.

Khaki, denim or outing flannel in shades of brown or gray will be suitable for all three garments. Lawn or batiste will serve for the undersleeves and the cravat. Buttons and buttonholes should be plain. Wooden button molds or cardboard will serve for the former, painted lines for the latter.

Long stockings of cotton or wool should be somber in color, the shoes black with bows of black ribbon or tape. The hat may be a woman's hat that is broad in the brim and low in the crown. A heavy cane would be an appropriate accessory.

Quaker women, like the men of that faith, were followers of current fashions but omitted extravagant trimmings. Soft gray, brown and plum were colors characteristic of the women's gowns although we read of green aprons and red cloaks. The fabrics used for neckerchiefs, caps and aprons were exceedingly fine, sheer and dainty.

Full skirts and aprons should both be made of straight pieces of muslin or plain chintz to represent soft silk. From four to five widths of cloth will be necessary for the skirt which should be gathered at the top and sewed to a close-fitting waistband.

For the darted bodice adapt a foundation waist pattern as

shown in Figure 47. Cut it either close about the neck or low, following the line indicated on the diagram. Edge the front with revers or a bias fold cut wide enough to give the desired effect. Sew on tapes with which to tie together the edges of the bodice along the front. Cut a triangle or a square of lawn

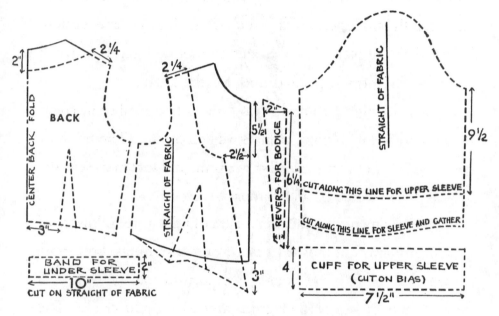

FIGURE 47. Bodice and Sleeve for Costume of Quaker Woman

or voile for the neckerchief. Make the undersleeves of lawn as described on page 67 and sew the lower edge of the sleeve into a close-fitting band.

For the hood cut black muslin or rayon taffeta in a semicircle whose straight edge measures thirty inches. Two and a half inches from the curved edge place several rows of running stitches and draw up the material to fit the neck. Baste a narrow ruffle of voile inside the straight edge of the hood.

Figure 48 illustrates the bonnet and shawl worn by the Quaker woman after the middle of the eighteenth century. For stage purposes these may be worn over a fitted bodice and full

FIGURE 48. A Quaker Bonnet and Shawl of 1860

skirt similar to those described on the preceding pages. The sleeves, however, should be long and finished with turned back cuffs of white. The pattern for the cuffs of the Puritan costume, page 78, may be used to cut these cuffs in white lawn or organdie.

AMERICAN DRESS IN THE
EIGHTEENTH CENTURY

FIGURE 49. Colonial Costumes, 1770

10. PRE-REVOLUTIONARY COSTUMES

Life was easier for the Colonists during the eighteenth century, both time and money being more abundant for most people. This permitted time and thought to be devoted to the demands of social intercourse, which in turn, required that considerable attention be given to matters of dress. Boston and Philadelphia were centers of fashion and in the museums of those cities we are able to study a great number of garments worn before the Revolutionary War.

Costume for men as well as women was, on the whole, gay and splendid. Rich velvets, satins, crisp silks, both flowered and plain, printed cottons and linens were quite generally worn by all people of social pretensions. Gold and silver braid, laces, plaitings, quiltings, ribbons and artificial flowers, jeweled buttons, and buckles contributed to the sparkle and gaiety of the costumes.

Early in the century when the hoop-skirt was adopted by women to hold out their spreading skirts, men began to wear the skirts of their coats stiffened with buckram. Soon the fronts of the coats were cut away to show more of the waistcoat as that long garment became increasingly decorative. The breeches were closer fitting than those worn in the earlier century and were fastened at the side of the knee with several buttons. The long stockings were white or a dark color and were worn under the breeches.

In the early part of the century the custom of powdering the hair was followed by both sexes, the men, in order to be in the height of fashion, adopting the wig. As the century advanced they caught the powdered locks at the back of the neck with a large bow of black ribbon.

Typical costumes worn just prior to the Revolutionary War are shown in Figure 49. In Figures 50 and 52 is indicated the method of adapting foundation patterns in order to obtain the close-fitting breeches, long coat and waistcoat. It is recommended that, as for the coat of the Quaker and the Colonist of Carolina, a pajamas coat pattern be used as the basic pattern. This will probably need a lengthwise tuck in both front and back to bring the armscye farther up on the shoulder and to make the entire coat fit more closely. Pin in a new underarm seam. Develop the back of the coat first allowing for plaits at

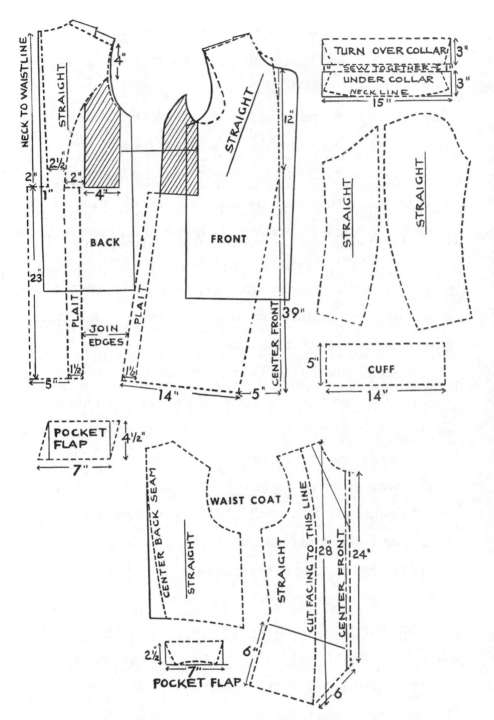

FIGURE 50. Coat and Waistcoat of Colonial Man, 1770

the center and side back seams. The side back of the coat pattern, indicated by the shading, should be pinned to the front of the coat along the underarm seam of the pattern. When cutting the coat from fabric cut along the dotted line of the shaded section so that there will be no seam directly under the arm. This was the method used in cutting this type of garment in the eighteenth century. If, however, the maker of the costume is not especially skilled in cutting and fitting, the front of the coat may be cut with an underarm seam, the side back section separately and then joined to the front with the regulation underarm seam and a seam at the waistline.

In order to have the coat fall properly on the wearer it is most essential that the fronts be cut with the grain as indicated in Figure 50. Place the pattern with the line marked *straight* parallel to the selvedge of the fabric.

The skirts of the coat should be interlined with a stiff canvas and the entire coat lined with a fabric of contrasting color. The collar and cuffs should also be interlined with canvas and the top of the cuffs caught to the sleeve under the buttons.

When cutting the collar cut two pieces for the turn-over section and two pieces for the collar section. One piece of canvas should be cut and used for the interlining of the collar section.

Inexpensive rayon satin or brocade will serve well for the waistcoat while the buttonholes and embroidery may be represented with gold radiator paint. The fronts of the waistcoat should be lined with paper cambric.

For the coat and breeches Canton flannel or heavy sateen should be satisfactory. Strips of mosquito netting will gather

FIGURE 51. Man's Coat, 1770

well and form satisfactory ruffles for sleeves and jabot. To make the latter cut a rectangle of the netting about twenty-four inches in length and ten inches in width. Round off all four corners, cut the edges in shallow scallops and gather the material through the center drawing it up until the desired length is obtained. Sew the jabot to a strip of netting long enough to wrap around the neck and to be pinned at the center back. It should be wide enough to crush softly.

To represent the large buttons of the coat cut circles of cardboard one and a half inches in diameter and paste over them

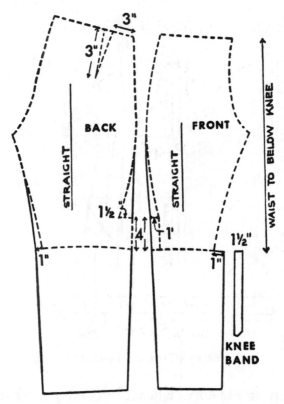

FIGURE 52. Man's Breeches, 1770

circles of similar size cut from the same material as is used for the coat, or paint the cardboard the desired color. Use small circles for the fastening of the breeches. For the jeweled buttons of the waistcoat follow the same procedure using circles three-quarters of an inch in diameter. In the center of each paste a smaller circle of colored cellophane.

For the large silver buckle on the man's shoe use cardboard or buckram painted with radiator paint or covered with tin foil. For the tongue of the shoe use black cambric or paper pasted to a piece of buckram cut the desired shape.

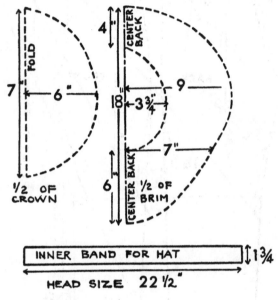

FIGURE 53. Tricorne Hat, 1770

Measurements for the tricorne hat characteristic of this period are given in Figure 53. Cut a paper pattern first and fit it properly to the head of the person to wear the costume. For the foundation brim use buckram cutting it according to the pattern, and with no seam allowance except at the inner circle. Next cut two thicknesses of black outing flannel for the brim

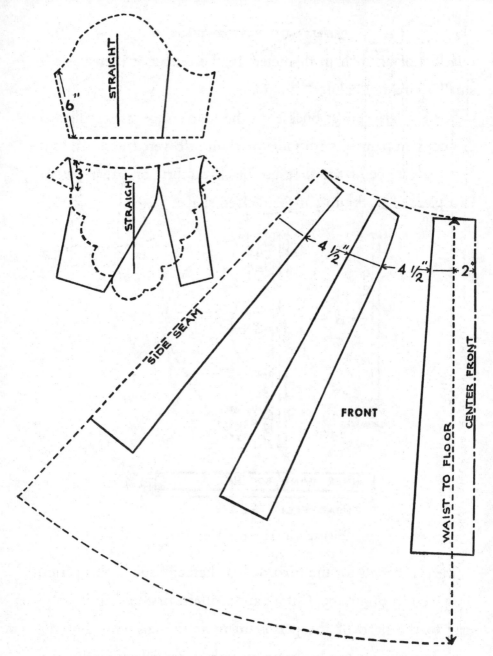

FIGURE 54. Watteau Gown (Front of Skirt and Sleeve), 1770

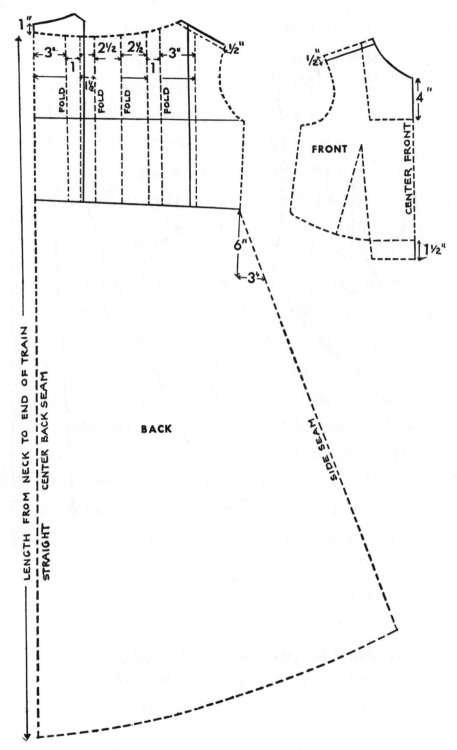

FIGURE 55. Watteau Gown (Back of Dress and Front of Bodice), 1770

allowing seams at the inner edges. Cover both sides of the buck-ram brim with the black cloth using milliner's glue or rubber cement to hold them together. For the crown cut one thickness of cloth and one of tarlatan. Pin both together and plait along the edge to fit the head size of the brim. Sew crown and brim together then sew both to the strip of cloth cut for the inside head-band. Turn up the brim in three places and tack it incon-spicuously to the crown.

Use cotton batting to represent the powdered hair making first in white cambric or tarlatan a close-fitting skullcap. Sew the cotton to this, arranging the cotton in two horizontal rolls above each ear and in one long lock to hang down the back beneath a black ribbon bow. White crepe hair may be used for the back hair if desired. Sew it to the base of the foundation and conceal the joining with the ribbon bow. The wig for the woman may be made in the same manner or the wearer's hair arranged in a pompadour in the front and a long curl over one shoulder. Talcum or cornstarch should be sprinkled on after the hair has been dressed.

The method of cutting the Watteau gown, so popular with Colonial women in the eighteenth century, is given in Figure 54. A plain shirtwaist pattern and the front and side front gores of a four-gored skirt are needed for this dress. The bodice front is exceedingly simple to construct as it consists of the usual shirtwaist front with the excess fullness at the waist removed by large darts on either side of the waist and concealed under the plaited trimming.

The cutting of the back of the gown is by no means formidable, once one understands that the extra allowance, inserted by

FIGURE 56. Back of Watteau Gown

slashing and spreading the back of a shirtwaist pattern, is to be stitched in two double box-plaits, one on each side of the center back seam as shown in Figure 55. It would be wise to make a trial pattern of this Watteau back, using tissue paper, fold the plaits as directed and hold it to the back of the person for whom the costume is to be made. Extra fullness, if needed, may then be inserted when cutting the fabric. It is essential that a close-fitting back of some lining material be made so that the side back of the gown may be sewed to it under the plait nearest the armscye and underarm. This will prevent the fullness billowing about and spreading awkwardly under the arm.

When the back has been cut mark clearly on the material the lines for the fold of each plait, fold as indicated in Figure 55 and stitch down along each fold two inches from the neckline. Pin the plaited back to the lining, then baste both to the front along the shoulder and underarm seams. Leave the center back seam open a sufficient number of inches to enable the wearer to get in and out of the dress. If preferred the dress may be left open at the left side of the center front and be fastened with small snaps under the plaited trimming.

The dress skirt should be open in the front to show the petti-coat, which in the Colonial period was so frequently quilted or embroidered. Figure 54 shows how to develop the front of the skirt from the gored pattern. The side front gore is slashed through the center and the three pieces of the pattern spread at the hip line approximately four and a half inches. The extra fullness at the waist should be laid in plaits to fit the front of the bodice to which the skirt is attached.

The petticoat may be made from three lengths of fabric

stitched together and plaited at the top to fit a snug waistband. Represent a quilted or embroided design by heavy, short lines in crayon.

The close-fitting short sleeve may be cut from the two-piece sleeve pattern, Figure 54, or from a shirtwaist sleeve pattern. The scalloped, circular ruffle is easily developed from the two-piece pattern. This ruffle should be made of the dress fabric and a similar piece of tarlatan or mosquito netting placed beneath it. Baste the ruffles to the end of the sleeve then cover the seam with a plaiting of the dress fabric. Cut the edges of the ruffles with a pinking shears to simplify the construction and to give, in addition, an authentic finish.

To make the box-plaited strips outlining the front edges of the skirt, the sleeves and the front of the waist, cut crosswise pieces of fabric with the pinking shears, if possible. The strips for the skirt should be four inches in width; those for the waist and sleeves should be two inches in width. Two inches from the end of a strip fold the material and by machine stitch three-fourths of an inch from the fold, forming a tuck. Two inches from the first fold stitch a second tuck then continue until sufficient lengths of material are prepared. Next press each tuck to form a small box-plait. Baste the trimming to the dress as shown in Figure 49.

Cotton prints, unglazed chintz, rayon taffeta or sateen are all inexpensive fabrics that may be used to represent the fabrics from which Colonial gowns were made.

As hoops were usually worn during the eighteenth century not only with the Watteau gown but with dresses of simpler cut, a hoop-skirt should be made for the wearer of this costume. A simple way to obtain the hoop-skirt is to sew six rows of half-inch wide tape, evenly spaced between the hem and waistlines

FIGURE 57. Hoops to be Worn Under Skirts of 1770 Costume

of a full, gored petticoat made of cambric. Sew the tapes along both edges then at the joining of each slip in a heavy wire cut two inches longer than the circumference of the part of the skirt where it is to be placed.

The hoop-skirt illustrated in Figure 57 is made of wires held together by lengths of tape that have been first stitched to a piece of tape that fits the waist of the wearer and has ends long enough to tie. Cut nine pieces of tape, each thirty-six inches long. Divide the tape for the belt into nine equal divisions and stitch the ends of the long tapes to the belt at the dividing points. Cut five pieces of wire, or featherboning, measuring 100 inches, 98 inches, 88 inches, 77 inches and 50 inches, respectively. Fasten the ends of the longest wire securely together, then pin the end of each long tape around the hoop of wire. Form hoops of the remaining wires and attach them to the lengthwise tapes until the frame is formed. Fasten each wire securely to the tapes.

Satin slippers with baby Louis or slightly higher heels should be worn with dresses of this period. A dainty folding fan will be appropriate to carry.

ILLUSTRATION 7. A Camlet Hood worn by women of all ranks and ages from about 1690-1750. A Colonial Quakeress would make it out of a drab fabric but line it with silk. The fashionable dames would make them out of gaily colored silk.

ILLUSTRATION 8. 1740's. Simple Headdresses worn by ladies. Some were trimmed with artificial flowers.

NOTE: Men still wore ribbons to tie their long hair or adorn their wigs.

Figure 58. Uniforms of the Revolutionary War

11. REVOLUTIONARY WAR UNIFORMS

Contemporary descriptions of the Continental Army when its command was taken over by General Washington picture it as clothed in a motley array of garments. The coats, waistcoats and breeches worn by the patriots were usually their own civilian clothing. It was difficult to get cloth or money for uniforms, but as the Continental Congress resolved at different times that clothing should be provided for the fighting forces, there slowly came into being a type of uniform that was similar in many ways to the civilian dress of the day.

During the early part of the war a hunting shirt of buck skin or linen, breeches and gaiters, large brimmed hat, ruffled shirt and black stock was the field service dress recommended by General Washington. As the war progressed the uniform consisting of blue cutaway coat, buff waistcoat, breeches or overalls came into existence, Figure 58. The facing and lining of the coat varied for different branches of the service and for regiments from different parts of the country. In October 1779 the Commanding General, on authority from Congress, directed that the coats of the soldiers from New Hampshire, Massachusetts, Rhode Island and Connecticut be blue with facings and linings, as well as buttons, of white; the coats of soldiers from New York and New Jersey be blue with facings of buff, and linings and buttons of white. The men from North and South Carolina and Georgia were to wear blue coats faced with blue, lined with white and fastened with buttons of white while soldiers from Pennsylvania, Maryland and Virginia were to have their blue coats faced with red, lined with white and fastened with buttons of white. Different military ranks were distinguished from each other by various epaulets and insignia as well as by feathers in their cocked hats.*

In Figure 58 are shown the hunting shirt uniform worn in 1774 and 1775, and the uniform worn from 1776 to 1779. To construct the hunting shirt, Figure 59, in khaki or tan outing flannel, use a pajamas coat pattern as the foundation, applying strips of the same cloth cut into fringe at the neck, armscye and elbows. The bottom of the shirt and the sleeves should also be cut into narrow slashes to simulate fringe.

* For exact descriptions and details the reader is referred to books dealing with uniforms as listed in the bibliography.

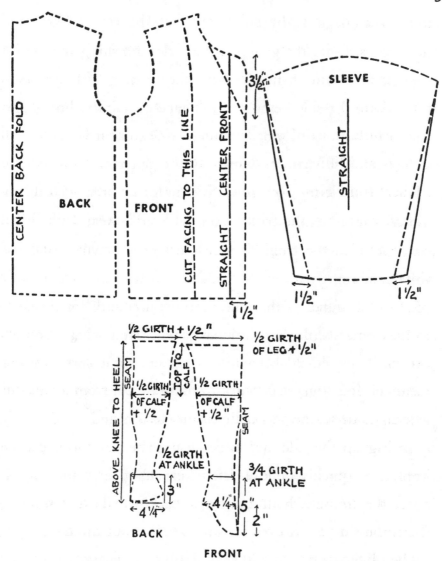

FIGURE 59. Jacket and Gaiters of the Soldier of the Revolutionary
War in 1774 and 1775

For the close-fitting breeches use the pattern shown on page
100 for the breeches of the men of 1770. Figure 59 suggests the
pattern to be used for cutting leggings in khaki. Obtain a close

fit for each legging by adjusting it at the center front and back seams. Close the gaiters at the sides, finishing them with one-half inch wide hems. To save the making of buttonholes stitch along the side hems strips of tape containing hooks and eyes. Sew buttons of wooden molds or cardboard on the top of the hem. Use khaki or flannel for the gaiters.

For the stock to accompany this uniform use a wide black ribbon fastened at the back of the neck, and wear with this a white shirt, to the front of which has been sewn a ruffle of white cambric.

Figure 60 indicates the modifications necessary for developing the overalls of the Revolutionary soldier from a basic trousers pattern. They should be made in tan or buff colored muslin or flannel. It is suggested that if trousers are cut from a pajamas pattern, made several inches longer in the legs and fitted closely by taking up the side and under leg seams, the work can be simply and quickly done. Darts taken along the center of the leg of the trousers, both front and back will be necessary to obtain the smooth fit over the instep and about the ankle.

The blue coat of the soldier is similar in general cut to that of the civilian of 1770. To develop the pattern for this coat follow the diagram, Figure 61. The facing pattern should be made by using the front of the coat pattern from the front edge to the dotted line indicating the inner edge of the facing.

The lining for the tails, which should be open at the center back from the waistline, should be cut exactly like the pattern for

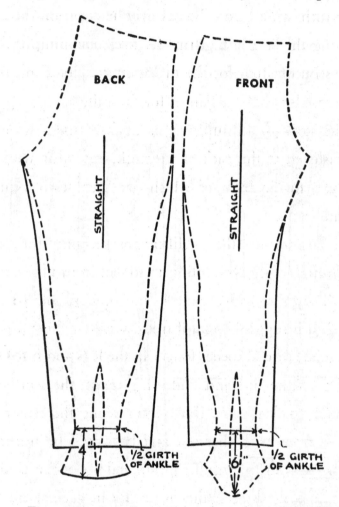

FIGURE 60. Overalls of the Revolutionary Soldier

the tails. Use muslin in the appropriate color for the lining. Cut the collar and cuffs from the same fabric as the coat facing and interline them with canvas. Catch the lower corners of the coat fronts to the corners of the tail ends at the center back with two buttons.

The waistcoat of buff or white may be cut from the modern vest. It should be cut high in the neck and finished with a straight strip of cloth for the upstanding collar.

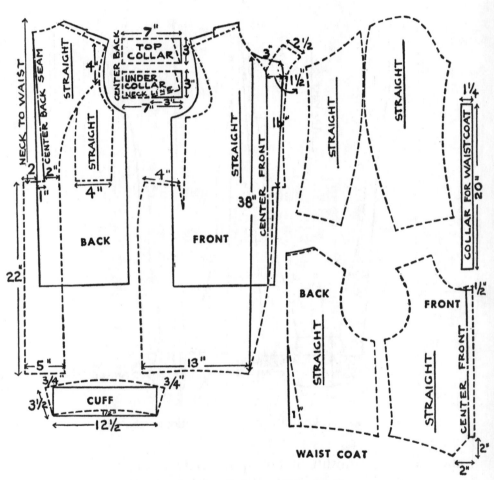

FIGURE 61. Revolutionary War Uniform

AMERICAN DRESS 1800-1870

FIGURE 62. Costumes of the Early Republic, 1804

12. 1800-1810

Examples of fashionable men's dress in the early years of the
nineteenth century may be seen in the portraits of political and
social leaders of the day. As yet the breeches had not been supplanted by the new fashioned pantaloons. The coats, dark blue,
brown or green, in color, were cut away in the front with tails
reaching barely to the knee. The extremely short front of the
coat, showing the gay waistcoat, was by 1806 somewhat longer,
and as a rule double-breasted. The coat collar was very high in
the back and at the sides. The revers were wide. About the neck
was wrapped a white cravat fastened at the front in a small
knot and two short ends. Below was the ruffled shirt front of
white cambric or linen.

The short waistcoats, single or double-breasted, were made
of satin or other light-colored fabrics, frequently striped as well
as quilted, and fastened with plated buttons.

While long, close-fitting trousers came into fashion in the early nineteenth century, breeches were still very generally worn, frequently with long boots. The breeches were very often of buff-colored fabric and fastened at the knee with small buttons. Stockings were light in color, white being extremely common. Slippers were thin in sole, low of heel and had a small buckle of silver at the instep. Hats were of beaver, high of crown and narrow of brim.

To cut the breeches for the 1804 costume shown in Figure 62 use the same foundation pattern employed to make the breeches for the costume of 1770, Figure 52. Simulate the pockets by stitching two strips of cloth five inches by one and a quarter inches in the position shown.

For the man's cutaway coat use as the foundation the pattern for a pajamas coat. Pin the pattern together, hold it to the wearer of the costume and, in order to make the coat close-fitting pin a tuck in the pattern, front and back, from shoulder to hem. On this fitted pattern block out the seam lines as indicated in Figure 63 varying the measurements as necessary to conform to the wearer's size. No plaits in the side back seams of the coat are shown in Figure 63, but if desired they may be arranged for when cutting the cloth. One and a half or two inches will be sufficient to allow for each plait.

As the front of the coat must be faced to form the revers, cut

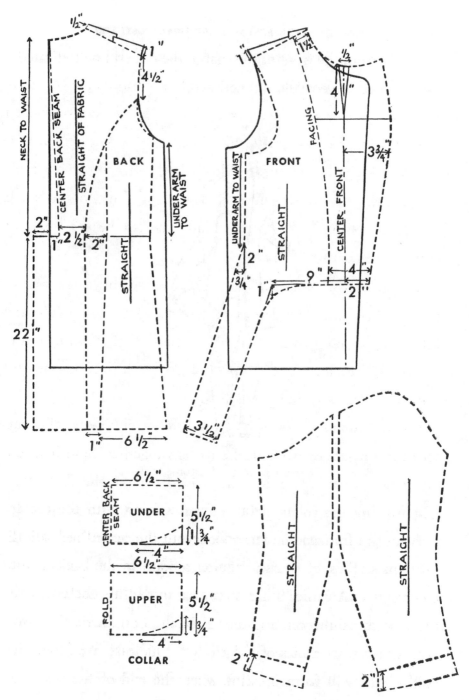

FIGURE 63. Man's Coat, 1804

the facing from the front of the coat to the dotted line indicated. The skirts of the coat should be lined.

FIGURE 64. Man's Costume, 1804

In making the collar cut the upper section with the center back along a fold, the under section with the center back along a true bias. This, of course, requires a seam in the back of the under collar. An interlining of canvas should also be cut with a bias seam at the center back. Face the bottom of the two-piece sleeve with a bias of the cloth cut at least five inches in width. This will form the cuff when the end of the sleeve is turned back.

For the stock use a strip of cambric or fine cheesecloth six inches wide and approximately forty inches long. To a white shirt front baste a two-inch strip of cambric gathered or plaited to form a ruffle.

White silk stockings and black pumps, such as are appropriate for evening wear today, should be worn with this costume.

Tan muslin of heavy quality will serve for the fabric of the breeches, while drilling or inexpensive cotton gabardine may be used for the coat. If a short waistcoat is to be worn use a printed stripe cotton or plain sateen of a bright color.

In the early nineteenth century the Paris vogue for scant, sheer dresses and little underwear was followed by women in this country with much enthusiasm. Waistlines were very high, just under the breasts, sleeves very short and full for evening but long and fairly tight for street wear. In evening dresses the necklines were round and extremely low. For daytime wear the bodices were cut high, to the normal neckline and finished with a turned-down collar or a standing collar edged at the top with a narrow ruching. Some of the afternoon dresses had low necklines filled in with guimps or kerchiefs. For all dresses the skirts were extremely scant, consisting of three or four breadths of the eighteen or twenty-seven inch wide fabric of the day. Practically all skirts reached to the ankles, the evening gown only having a slight train.

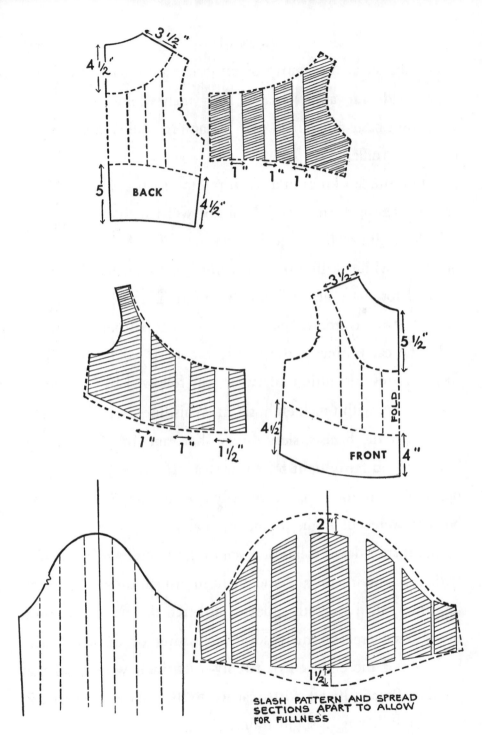

FIGURE 65. Woman's Dress, 1804

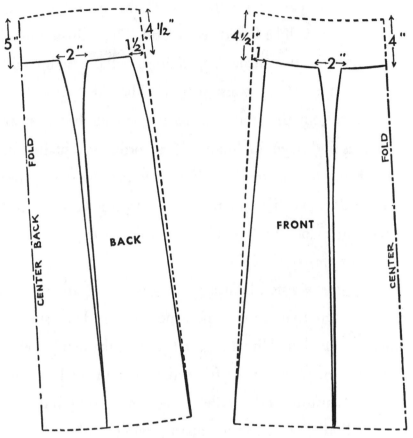

FIGURE 66. Woman's Dress, 1804

In making up costumes for this period use such soft, clinging materials as heavy cheesecloth, inexpensive batiste, net or sateen and wear under the dresses long, narrow slips of silk or rayon so that the dress will not cling to the body in an unattractive manner. White dresses were most popular but as we read that silks of every color were prevalent, cheesecloth or thin muslin in various colors will not be inappropriate.

To obtain the pattern for the skirt of this period a six-gore foundation skirt will be found very useful. The waistline should be raised four or five inches depending on the amount taken from the bottom of the waist pattern. The side gores should be separated from the front and back gores at the waist and hip lines as indicated in Figure 66 in order to obtain some fullness in the top of the skirt. If a pattern for a street-length dress is used extend the pattern to reach to the wearer's ankle. A measurement of fifty-four to sixty inches at the hem line is sufficient for this type of skirt.

For the short-waisted bodice use a shirtwaist pattern as the foundation. On that draw a new neckline and waistline as indicated by the dotted lines, Figure 65. Slash the newly formed pattern in three places in the front and three in the back from neckline to waistline and parallel to the center front and center back lines. Spread these sections apart leaving one inch between the sections, and pin to paper or directly to the dress fabric. With pins or chalk mark continuous lines for the neck and waistlines, then cut the front and back of the bodice. Take up the fullness just added by gathering along the neck and waist-lines. Draw up the gathers to fit the wearer. If desired turn and stitch a three-eighths inch hem at the neckline, after sewing up the shoulder seams, and draw a narrow tape through the hem. The fullness can then be easily adjusted on the wearer.

Gather the top of the skirt and join it to the waistline of the bodice. This dress should open along the center back.

FIGURE 67. Back of Woman's Dress, 1804

The Empire puff sleeve should be developed in a manner similar to that used for inserting fullness in the front and back of the bodice. Using a one-piece foundation sleeve pattern cut in paper a sleeve that is four inches in length at the under seams. Slash the paper sleeve six times and place on the fabric, spreading the sections until the desired amount of fullness is obtained. Throw more fullness through the center of the sleeve than under the arm. Extend the upper and lower curves as indicated and cut the sleeve from the fabric. Finish the bottom of the sleeve with a narrow hem and in it insert a round elastic to fit the girth of the arm.

As the silk or soft kid slippers of this period were heelless the wearer of this costume should use pullman, ballet or other very flat-heeled slippers as foot covering. A fairly good substitute slipper may be made from felt or paper cambric by using the Indian moccasin pattern, Figure 16, as a foundation, omitting the cuffs and cutting the upper to look like the slipper in Figure 62. The sole should be cut from buckram or drilling.

Arrange the hair in ringlets about the face and use a narrow ribbon for the fillet. As short hair was fashionable at this period the wearer whose own hair is cut short need not feel that her hair arrangement is inappropriate for the period represented.

Caps of muslin and lace were made in a variety of styles while the hats invariably were adorned with one or more ostrich plumes. Another favorite headdress of the period was a length of silk or printed cotton fabric wrapped about the head like a turban. An upstanding plume was placed at the front of the turban.

The poke bonnet of the day may be simulated by using a straw hat with a moderately wide brim and sewing to the sides of the crown, on the top of the hat, fairly broad ribbons that are to be tied under the chin.

Colored rather than white kid gloves were much worn by early nineteenth century women and a "ridicule" or handbag was considered indispensable. A typical bag is shown in Figure 62.

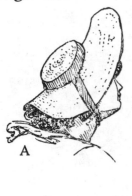

ILLUSTRATION 9. 1800-1810.
A. Gypsy hat, 1800-1810.   B. Cap trimmed with Amaranthus Crepe, locket watch, 1800.   C. Velvet turban with a "banditti" plume and a veil hanging to the shoulders, 1801.   D. Lavinia hat of straw, 1807.   E. Straw bonnet with silk crown to be worn over a cap, 1806.

FIGURE 68. Costumes Worn in 1835

13. 1820-1840

The Beau Brummels of the 1820s and 1830s were colorfully clad in cutaway coats, elaborate waistcoats, high stocks, the usual ruffled shirt and in trousers which finally crowded out the knee-length breeches that had been fashionable for more than a century. Dark as well as light colors were used for the trousers which, in general, reached down over the shoe. After 1830, when trousers became very close fitting, straps were passed under the shoe to hold the trousers down.

The collars of the men's white shirts were exceedingly high showing above the top of the wide, dark silk stock wound about the throat.

For the trousers shown in Figure 68 the regulation pajamas pattern may be used. Fit the trousers snugly about the waist by taking in darts and a deeper seam along the side. If the trousers of the 1830s are to be represented fit them rather closely

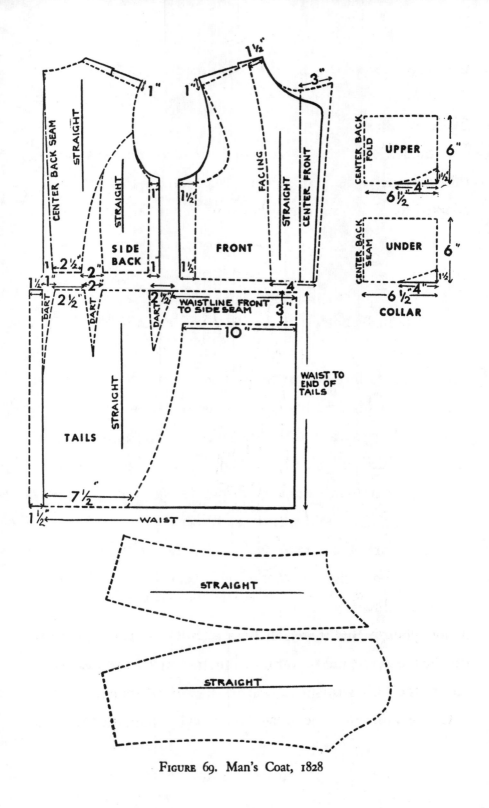

FIGURE 69. Man's Coat, 1828

their entire length and at the bottom sew a one-inch wide strap that is to be passed under the wearer's shoe in gaiter fashion. Elastic may be used if desired.

A modern vest will furnish the pattern for the waistcoat of this costume, while the pajamas coat pattern can be readily adapted for the coat pattern shown in Figure 69. Fit the foun-

FIGURE 70. Back of Man's Suit, 1828

dation pattern to the wearer as suggested on page 96, then use the measurements on the diagram, modifying them as necessary to meet the requirements of the individual figure.

Cut two pieces of the fabric for the collar and cut the front facing as far as the dotted line on the diagram. The tails of the coat should be lined.

Cut a strip of white paper cambric two inches wide and crosswise of the material, press it into small plaits and baste it to the front of the white shirt to be worn with the costume. Use a four or five inch strip of the same cambric or black ribbon for the stock.

Light gray or tan cotton gabardine will be found satisfactory material for the trousers, sateen for the waistcoat and blue, black or brown denim for the coat. A fairly heavy cotton must be used to give the effect of the broadcloths and other fine fabrics of that day.

The fashions in women's dress during the 1820s and 1830s were extreme in silhouette and on the whole the dresses were very much overtrimmed. Skirts were fairly short, reaching to the ankles and very full at the hem line which was accentuated with crosswise tucks, folds, ruffles and other decorations. The sleeves were voluminous at the top and set into a lowered armscye. By 1835 the sleeve fullness had dropped to the elbow and the skirts of evening gowns touched the floor. The horizontal movement was, however, still dominant. Bows of ribbon, flowers, folds and flounces were still the chief form of decoration. Taffeta, satin, gauze, chintz, cashmere, watered silk, India muslin are fabrics we read about in the fashion magazines of

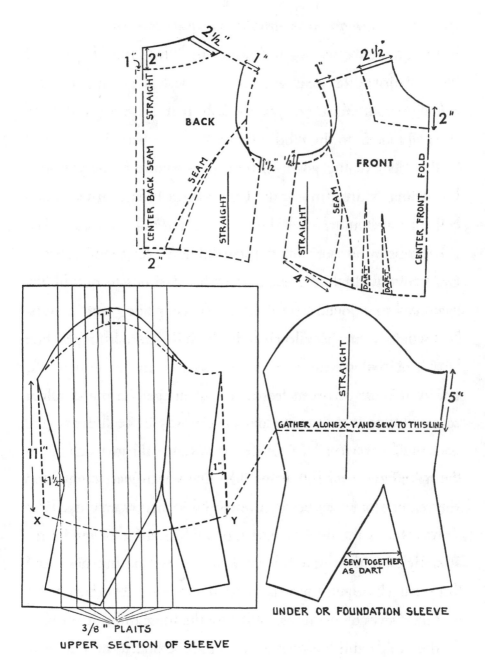

FIGURE 71. Woman's Bodice and Sleeves, 1835

these years. Lace scarves and cashmere shawls were apparently great favorites for wear with the low-necked gowns. The extremely small waistlines played their part in giving the hour glass silhouette to the modish women of the period.

The silk evening gown illustrated in Figure 68 is typical of the woman's dress in 1835. By wearing a broad turned down collar or a shoulder cape the same design will serve as a daytime dress to be worn on the stage. The skirt should be made from four widths of a suitable fabric to simulate one of the materials mentioned above. It should be plaited into a waist belt which in turn should be attached to the close-fitting bodice.

If a shirtwaist pattern is to be used for the pattern of the bodice it must be cut at least one inch longer on the shoulder seams. Darts in front and diagonal seams in both front and back will remove all fullness at the waist and give the tight-fitting effect required. The folds across the chest and down the center front may be represented by a narrow tape dyed the same color as the dress material, or by bias strips of the fabric. Rickrack braid of suitable color will serve for the neck and sleeve finish. Open the waist and skirt down the center back.

The sleeves of the dress constitute the most difficult problem of the design. Figure 71 illustrates the method to be followed. First lay in the fabric nine lengthwise plaits, each one three-eighths of an inch in depth. Press the plaits lightly. Cut the fabric using a two-piece sleeve pattern as indicated. Hold the plaits in position at the top of the sleeve with two rows of tape or folds of the fabric stitched directly over the plaits. See Figure 68. Gather the bottom of the sleeve. Cut an under sleeve with a

FIGURE 72. Woman's Dress, 1835

dart from the wrist to the elbow. Place the bottom of the plaited upper sleeve five inches down from the top of the foundation or under sleeve and stitch the two together along the line of gathering. Baste the two sleeves together at the top before placing in the armscye.

A strip of black or white mosquito netting eighty-four inches long and twenty-four inches wide will make a good substitute for a lace scarf. Cut scallops along the edge and with crayon draw in lines to make a pattern or design.

If the wearer of the 1835 costume has bobbed hair, switches of hair curled in the manner shown in Figure 68 may be pinned or tied to her own hair. If switches cannot be obtained form the curls from crepe hair shaped over a curling iron.

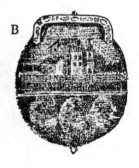

ILLUSTRATION 10. 1820-40. A. 1835. Artificial curls fastened to a comb. B. 1820-40. Beaded purse. C. 1835. Bonnet.

14. 1840-1850

Waistcoats of striking texture, color and pattern seemed to characterize the dress of an American gentleman of the 1840s. Plaids, stripes and all over designs of flowers in silk brocades and velvets added their color note to the dark frock coat and the light, high silk hat in which every well-dressed man considered it necessary to appear. In the late 1840s the white waistcoat became extremely popular.

The white shirt ruffle was discarded when a huge cravat of silk crowded the space above the top of the waistcoat with its roll collar and the high, sharply pointed white collar of the shirt itself. A gleaming stickpin ornamented the knot of the cravat.

The coat of 1847, Figure 73, is long both front and back with very large revers. The collar, too, is high. It must be cut in two pieces, an under collar and an upper collar, and in order

FIGURE 73. Costumes Worn in 1847

to roll properly the under collar should be interlined with canvas. Cut both under collar and the interlining with the center back as a bias seam. The side back seams of the coat have one and a half inch plaits. Any dark, fairly heavy cotton fabric may be used for the coat.

The waistcoat pattern is very similar to that of waistcoats worn by men today. The rolling collar pattern is shown on the pattern for the front of the waistcoat, Figure 74. Cut this from two thicknesses of fabric and join to the waistcoat at the neck line. It will not be necessary to cut the back of the collar as it will not show under the high-cut coat collar.

As waistcoat buttons w re bright and colorful in the 1840s use inexpensive buttons or cut small circles from gilt-covered or painted cardboard and paste in the center small pieces of colored cellophane.

For the high shirt-collar use a man's collar that is not very stiffly starched. A large colored handkerchief may be folded along the bias and arranged in the manner shown in Figure 73.

Cut the trousers from light-colored suede cloth or cotton gabardine using a pajamas or other trousers pattern. Fit the trousers rather closely at the bottom if the character to be represented was a man who dressed in the height of fashion. Along the side seams sew black tape one inch in width.

In the mid '40s cashmere, muslin, changeable silks, moiré,

challis and tarlatan were among the favorite materials for the
women's dresses. Practically all gowns were very full in the
skirt and tight-fitting in the bodice. The front of the bodice

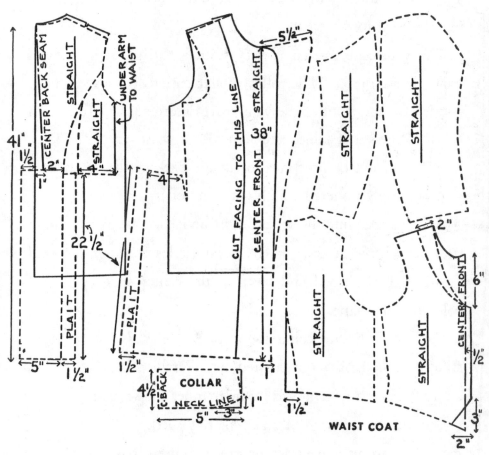

FIGURE 74. Man's Coat and Waistcoat, 1847

came over the skirt in a deep point. Sleeves for daytime wear
were long and very tight, the shoulders long and sloping. The
popular neckline for street dresses was square or round over

a chemisette finished at the neck with a small flat collar of lace or embroidery. The neckline for evening wear was round and low as shown in Figure 73.

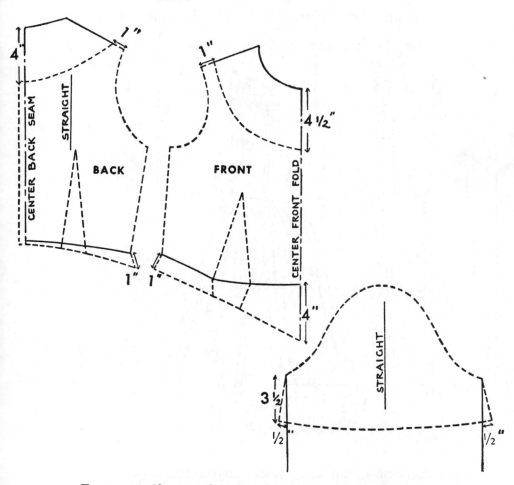

FIGURE 75. Sleeve and Bodice for Woman's Costume, 1847

The bodice of the dress illustrated is fitted at the waistline by means of darts, Figure 75, and opens at the center back. The sleeve is somewhat over three inches in length and finished at the edge, as is the neckline, with small ruching which can be made by plaiting strips of tarlatan or mosquito netting.

The skirt is made of straight pieces of cloth, four or five widths, plaited into a waist belt. The braiding on skirt and bodice may be indicated with heavy lines of crayon. Sateen,

FIGURE 76. Woman's Dress, 1847

paper cambric or an inexpensive rayon moiré would be very suitable for this type of gown. Some skirts had several rows of ruffles or wide flounces between the hip and waistlines.

As this was the era of many, many petticoats several skirts should be worn under this dress to give the effect of width

over the hips. A modified form of the sixteenth century farthingale might be worn in lieu of the many petticoats. See page 62.

The hair-dressing of the period is very easy to imitate. False
curls made of crepe hair can be pinned or tied to the hair above
the ears, and a knot or braid of hair arranged at the back.

Bonnets of the period were of the modified poke bonnet
type with ruchings, feathers and lace the popular trimming.
Deep shoulder capes of silk or fur with long ends in front
were worn on the street with these costumes.

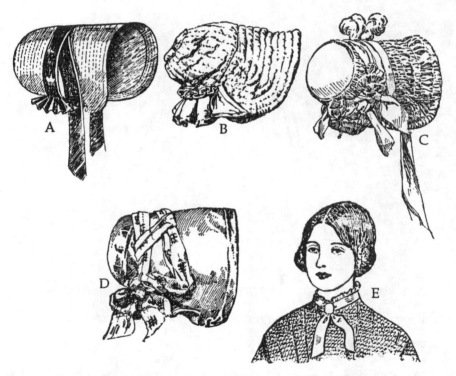

ILLUSTRATION 11. 1840-50. A. 1840. Plain straw bonnet trimmed with
ribbon. B. 1845. Quilted hood of ruby silk. C. 1847. Bonnet of shirred
white satin with "panache" of ostrich tips. D. 1848. Bonnet of satin with
ribbons for trim. E. 1840-48. Hair in Polish Braids.

Figure 77. Costumes Worn in 1860's

15. 1850-1870

While the swallow-tail coat with white waistcoat was fashionable in the decade before the Civil War it was gradually supplanted, particularly for daytime wear, by the frock coat of glistening black broadcloth. The trousers were generously cut, the waistcoat, straight across the front and double-breasted and with deep revers, was still of a cloth that contrasted in color and texture with the other garments. Figured fabrics as well as black satin were extremely popular. The shirt retained its high collar but the huge cravat was replaced by a large necktie tied in a rather negligent manner. The foppish element in men's attire had entirely disappeared by 1860. When comparing the coat shown in Figure 77 with that shown in Figure 73 it will be seen that the very large revers and collar that characterized men's coats in 1847 were decidedly modified in 1860.

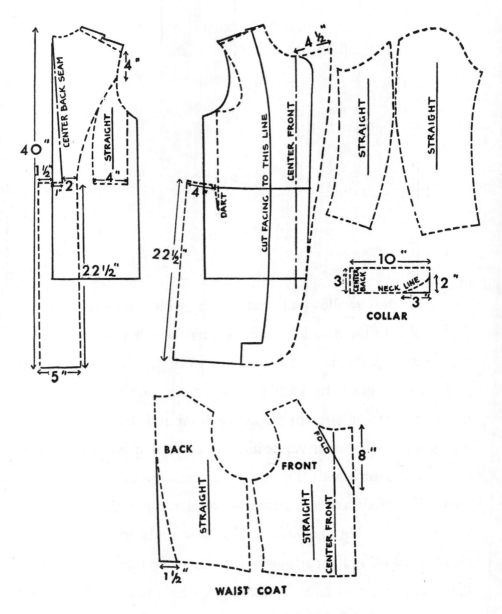

FIGURE 78. Man's Coat and Waistcoat, 1860

The pattern for the coat of the 1860s is shown in Figure 78, the back consisting of the long center section, open from the waist down, and the side back section reaching to a rather low waistline. The skirt of this frock coat is joined to the side back and front sections with a plain seam. As in the case of all other coats for men, it is suggested that this pattern be developed from a pajamas coat pattern.

The waistcoat is very easily constructed from the modern vest. By cutting the fronts at least two and a half inches beyond the center line of the pattern the double-breasted effect and the large revers will be obtained. The fronts of the waistcoat must be faced with the fabric used for the waistcoat.

A pair of modern dark cloth trousers will serve to wear with this frock coat provided the trousers are large from the hips down. A long strip of paper cambric or sateen wound about the throat and tied in the type of bow shown in Figure 77 will serve for the neck finish of this costume.

To represent the beards, whiskers and mustaches of this period use crepe hair. First apply to the face with a small brush a coating of spirit gum, then apply small amounts of the crepe hair trimming it to the shape and form desired.

While women's dresses in the 1860s were tight in the bodice and full in the skirt, as were those in the 1840s, there the similarity ends. Shoulder lines became somewhat longer and their breadth was accentuated by broad berthas. Sleeves were of three-quarter length and cut extremely broad about the waist and hips. Puffed undersleeves of embroidered batiste showed beneath the widely flaring sleeves of the dress.

Skirts were cut with almost the same fullness at the waist as at the hem, plaited or gathered into a waistband and distended by the hoop-skirt worn beneath. About 1860 the hoop-skirt replaced the broad band of crinoline, a stiff, flexible material, at the bottom of the dress skirts. Crosswise ruffles were very much in favor as they added so much to the desired silhouette.

Moiré silks, crisp taffetas, fine, smooth wool materials as well as cambrics, muslins and calicoes were the favorite fabrics for the bouffant gowns.

Brooches were usually worn at the neck and, for evening, especially, a band of black velvet encircled the throat.

Hats of silk or straw were very small, of the bonnet type and generously trimmed with ribbons, plaitings and feathers. Shoes had high tops and heels of considerable height.

In constructing a costume of this period cut the bodice from a shirtwaist pattern increasing the shoulder length at least one inch and removing the fullness at the waist by several darts. Drop the waist all around below the normal waistline, as much as three inches in the front. For the pagoda sleeve spread a two-piece sleeve pattern two or more inches at the elbow line

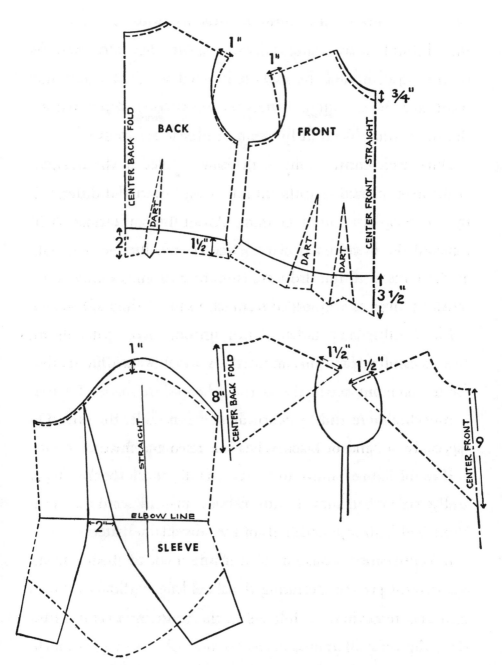

FIGURE 79. Bodice, Sleeve and Yoke for Woman's Costume, 1860

along the back seam and shape the lower edge as desired. As the shoulder line of the dress is lowered one inch, that same amount must be removed from the top curve of the sleeve.

The bertha shown in Figure 77 is developed from the front and back of a simple waist pattern as illustrated in the diagram, Figure 79. Both bertha and bodice should open along the center front. Black or white mosquito netting or tarlatan will serve as the lace with which the dress is trimmed.

As skirts of this period were from four to six yards in width at the hem, four or more lengths of thirty-six inch-wide fabric should be stitched together, slightly gored at the top if desired, and plaited to fit a belt about the normal waist. The bodice need not be sewed to the skirt. A hoop-skirt made of wires, featherboning or stiff reeds should be worn under the skirt. On page 108 are given the directions for making such a hoop-skirt.

For the bonnet shown in Figure 77 the pattern for the Dutch and Quaker bonnets, Figure 41, page 79, will serve as a general guide. Place a ruffle cut on the bias of the material at the neck edge of the bonnet and a ruching made of plaited net at the front to frame the face and parted hair. Buckram covered with sateen or rayon taffeta will have the stiffness required for the shape of this bonnet.

16. CIVIL WAR UNIFORMS

As every school child knows blue and gray were the colors of the uniforms worn in the American Civil War. The enlisted man of the Northern armies wore a dark blue sack coat with a narrow turned-down collar, light blue trousers, dark blue blouse and light blue overcoat. This latter garment had a deep cape which reached to the cuff of the sleeve and was faced with the color which indicated the branch of the service to which he was attached, scarlet for the artillery, yellow for the engineers and sky blue for the infantry. On his forage cap were the regimental number and corps device.

The officer's uniform consisted of dark blue coat, trousers and overcoat. The frock coat was double-breasted, fastened with two rows of buttons and had a narrow standing collar. Shoulder straps denoted the wearer's rank and the color of the welting in the side seam of the trousers indicated the arm of the service

FIGURE 80. Uniforms of Civil War Officer and Private

to which he belonged. The overcoat was fastened across the front by four frogs. A black felt hat, with the proper insignia, high boots, gauntlet gloves, broad belt and saber completed the uniform of the Northern officer.

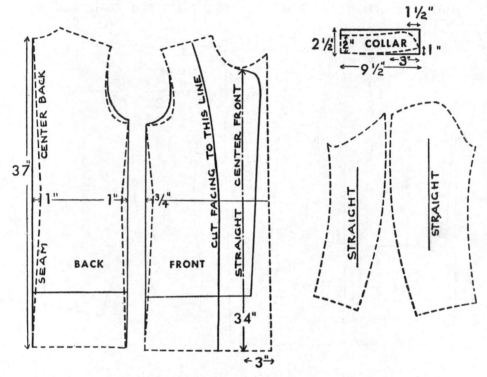

FIGURE 81. Coat of Civil War Officer

In the Confederate Army the uniforms were gray throughout. For both officers and men the coat was double-breasted, the rank of the officer being designated by the appropriate number of knots of gold braid worn on the sleeve from cuff to elbow, and by stars embroidered in gold on the collar.

The method of adapting the pajamas coat pattern for the Northern officer's frock coat is shown in Figure 81. The same pattern may be used for the sack coat of the enlisted man by cutting the coat shorter, by allowing only one inch beyond the center front for the single-breasted coat, and by

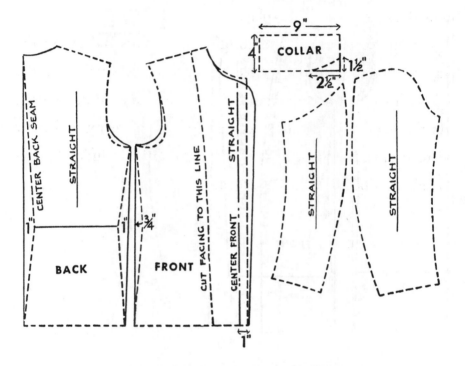

FIGURE 82. Tunic of Civil War Private

modifying the shape of the collar so that it turns down over the coat. Figure 82.

Dark blue serge trousers worn by the men of today will be acceptable for the uniform trousers. Baste a welt or strip of color on the side seams of the officer's trousers.

If a forage hat cannot be borrowed for the occasion one can be made with cardboard for the visor and the same cloth as that used for the coat will be appropriate for the round crown and the side section.

The accouterments of the soldiers should be borrowed or rented for the day of the play.

For the correct details of insignia and colors indicating the various branches of the service engaged in the Civil War the books listed in the bibliography will be found most helpful. As the regulations relating to uniforms of the army and navy were frequently changed it is not possible to include the full details in a book of this character.

APPENDIX

17. MATERIALS

In amateur plays of all kinds inexpensive productions are, of course, very essential. The fabrics for costumes, in addition to being pleasing in color and appropriate in texture, must be inexpensive. Typical fabrics which have proved satisfactory for costume purposes are unbleached muslin, sateen, khaki, cotton gabardine and denim for the heavier textures, inexpensive qualities of lawn and batiste for those of lighter weight. Cotton flannels, such as Canton, outing and flannelette, as well as suede cloth make excellent substitutes for velvets and skins. Cheesecloth has a clinging, sticking quality that, as a rule, renders it undesirable for most costumes unless a very heavy quality is used. Paper cambric is, on the whole, too light in weight for most costumes but is quite usable for linings, trimmings and petticoats.

When very sheer, lace-like effects are desired cotton lining net, mosquito netting and tarlatan usually answer the purpose.

For simulating the rich, heavy textures worn during the seventeenth century such fabrics as rayon brocade and rayon taffeta, glazed chintz, either plain or with printed designs give excellent results. If rayon satin is to be used for a period costume as dull a luster as possible should be purchased. Remnants of upholstery fabrics will make splendid waistcoats for men's costumes of the seventeenth and eighteenth centuries. To represent figured fabrics of rich, large design muslin and paper cambric can be easily painted or stenciled with show card colors.

Canvas and buckram will be found necessary for stiffening collars and hats, particularly. For trimmings upholstery braid, colored tapes of various widths, button molds and cellophane are all useful. White shelf paper can be used for collars and cuffs that require lace edging. It is, however, too fragile to be used more than once.

To calculate the amount of material to be bought for a given costume lay the various pieces of the pattern on newspapers that have been pinned together to represent a long length of cloth. The newspapers should be cut the width of the material that is to be used, approximately thirty-six inches for most cottons. Place the sections of the pattern as they should be placed on cloth with the lines marked "straight of material" parallel to the edge of the paper. Usually some sections must be placed on a lengthwise fold. Leave space between the sections for hem and seam allowances. When all pieces of the pattern have been placed measure the space occupied by the pattern as the amount of cloth to be purchased.

Cheap costume jewelry is always effective on the stage. The wooden beads used by young children as well as macaroni and spaghetti colored with oil paints make excellent stage accessories. Tin foil and radiator paint are useful for covering cardboard to represent buckles, pins and buttons of metal. Small pieces of colored cellophane or gum drops give the effect of jewels.

18. DYEING

As most inexpensive fabrics used for costume purposes are of cotton a dyestuff that is suitable for that fiber should be purchased. If rayon material is to be dyed special dyestuffs will be required if the rayon is of the acetate type. A simple way to determine whether or not the rayon is acetate is to touch the point of a hot iron to a corner of the material. Acetate rayon will melt under the heat.

As a general rule fabric should be dyed in the piece before the costume is cut and made. For greater ease in handling it is wise to measure and cut the length that will be required for one costume and dye that short length. Large quantities of cloth are always difficult to handle, require very large kettles and are likely to be streaked.

Mix the dye powder in a cup, dissolving the powder in hot water, then strain the liquid through a piece of cheesecloth directly into the kettle containing the right amount of cold water. Be sure to use a kettle that is large enough to hold a quantity of dye liquid that will completely cover the material without crowding it. Wet the material before immersing it in the dyebath. Turn the cloth constantly so that no part of it rests on the bottom of the container for any length of time. Sufficient dye liquid and constant stirring are absolutely necessary to the avoidance of streaks. Great care should be taken when dyeing rayon fabrics as that fiber loses strength when wet.

Bring the dyebath gradually to the boiling point and keep it at that point for fifteen minutes. If the directions that accompany the dyestuff call for the addition of salt add the stated amount and continue to boil the liquid for fifteen or twenty minutes. It is usually wise to remove the fabric from the kettle before the salt is added. If a deeper color is desired remove the fabric and add more dissolved dyestuff to the liquid. Remember that when the fabric is dry the color will be lighter and that grayed colors will look faded and muddy under the footlights. Strong, clear colors are desirable for stage costumes.

Rinse the material several times until the rinse water is perfectly clear. When the fabric is partly dry press carefully with the straight thread of the material. Rayon fabrics should not be wrung but allowed to drip. When napped fabrics have been dyed the napped surface should be brushed with a stiff whisk-broom.

If a colored fabric is to be redyed better results will usually be obtained if the original color is first stripped from it. Place the fabric in hot water and soap and boil it for several minutes, then change the water and repeat the process until all of the color has been removed.

19. CONSTRUCTION

In the making of costumes it should be remembered that effect is the prime requisite and that fine technique is not essential. Costumes should, of course, be well enough sewed to hold together for several performances. Seam allowances should be rather generous, particularly if the material tends to fray easily along the cut edges. As no seam allowance is calculated for the patterns suggested in the preceding pages it may not be amiss to state here that one and a half inches should be a safe allowance for all straight seams and three-eighths for all curved seams. Seam edges should not be finished. Hems should be turned once and stitched or lightly basted. Materials may be quickly gathered by placing the stitch regulator on a lock stitch machine at six stitches to the inch, and placing two rows of stitching three-eighths of an inch apart in the section to be gathered. Draw up the two under threads of the stitching at the same time.

The fronts and tails of the men's coats should be lined and the collars stiffened with canvas to give the proper effect. Only the buttonholes that will be actually used need to be cut. The others may be indicated with crayon, paint or tape.

Large hooks and eyes will be found more trustworthy than snaps for costumes. All fastenings should be placed where they can be easily manipulated by the wearer of the costume unless there are plenty of assistants on hand to dress the performers.

All garments should be carefully cut and fitted. They should be well pressed before each performance. Costumes made of rayon fabric should be pressed with a cool iron.

BIBLIOGRAPHY

COSTUME

Blakeslee, F. G. *Uniforms of the World* (New York, 1929).

Brooke, I. and Landes, William-Alan. *Western European Costume* 13th to 17th Centuries (Studio City, 1993).

Curtis, E. S. *The North American Indian* (Cambridge, 1907-1925).

Davis, R. I. *Men's Costume, Cut and Fashion of the 17th and 18th Centuries* (Studio City, 1994).

Earle, A. M. *Two Centuries of Dress in America* (New York, 1903).

Evans, Mary. *Costume Throughout the Ages* (Philadelphia, 1930).

Gummere, A. M. *The Quaker* (Philadelphia, 1911).

Hodge, F. W. *Handbook of the American Indian* (Washington, 1915).

Hoes, R. G. *Catalogue of American Historical Costumes* (Washington, 1915).

Hunnisett, J. *Period Costumes for Stage and Screen 1500-1800* (Studio City, 1991). *Period Costumes for Stage and Screen 1800-1909* (Studio City, 1991).

Lester, K. M. and Kerr, R. N. *Historic Costume* (Peoria, 1961).

McClellan, E. *History of American Costume* (Philadelphia, 1910).

Nelson, H. L. *The Army of the United States* (The Quartermaster's Office, Washington, 1889).

Singleton, E. *Social Life Under the Georges* (New York, 1902).

Spears, J. H. *History of Our Navy* (New York, 1897).

Verril, A. H. *The American Indian* (New York, 1927).

Warwick, E. and Pitz, H. C. *Early American Costume* (New York, 1929). Revised (New York, 1965).

Wharton, A. H. *Colonial Days and Dames* (Philadelphia, 1895). *Social Life in the Early Republic* (Philadelphia, 1902).

Wissler, Clark. *North American Indians of the Plains* (New York, 1912). *Indian Costumes in the United States* (New York, 1926).

DYES AND DYEING

Exmouth, C. E. P. *Dyes and Dyeing* (New York, 1928).

Pellew, C. E. *Dyes and Dyeing* New York, 1918).

Phillips, Martha J. *Modern Home Dyeing* (New York, 1922).

Powers, Janet. *Manual on Home Tinting and Dyeing* (New York, 1936).

Wiltern, T. E. *Theatrical Fabric Magic* (Sidney, 1984).

MAKE-UP

Jans, M. and Landes, William-Alan. *Stage Make-Up Techniques* (Studio City, 1993).

Morton, C. *The Art of Theatrical Make-up* (London, 1909).

MAGAZINES

Ladies' Magazine, 1829-1834.
Godey's Lady's Book, 1830-1877.
Peterson's Magazine, 1842-1898.
Lady's Wreath of New York, 1846-1855.
Frank Leslie's Lady's Magazine, 1852-1857.

AMERICAN PAINTERS WHOSE WORKS SHOW COSTUME

Benbridge, H.

Blackburne, J.

Boughton, G. H.

Copley, J. S.

Huntington,, D.

Morse, S. F. B.

Peale, C. W.

Pratt, M.

Pyne, T.

Stuart, G.

Sulley, T.

Trumbull, J.

Vanderlyn, J.

West, B.

INDEX

Other Costume Books from PLAYERS PRESS

Available 1994

MEN'S GARMENTS 1830-1900 (Revised Second Edition)

by R. I. Davis. Book includes drawn to scale patterns for historically accurate costumes and instructions on cutting, plus tailoring secrets necessary to make these garments look authentic.

Not available in the U.S.A.

160 pgs   pb   8 1/2 x 11   ISBN 1-85729-020-8

MEN'S COSTUME, CUT AND FASHION 17th and 18th Century

by R. I. Davis

Tremendously well researched and exquisitely drawn guide to men's costume and construction. Patterns are historically correct and drawn to scale. A must for every costumer!

hc   8 1/2 x 11   ISBN 0-88734-637-5

PERIOD COSTUME FOR STAGE & SCREEN 1300-1500

by Jean Hunnisett. The exciting new addition to her Period Costume series. Drawn-to-scale patterns and techniques for accurate duplication of classic costumes for women. Patterns have already been adapted to fit the modern-day female form. An invaluable resource for amateur and professional costumers. **due Fall/Winter 1994**

hc   8 1/2 x 11   ISBN 0-88734-643-X

THE ART OF BEDOUIN JEWELLERY A Saudi Arabian Profile

A magnificent book detailing the culture, craft and fashion of Arabian and Bedouin jewelry. A perfect companion to THE ART OF ARABIAN COSTUME.

hc   133 pgs   10 1/4 x 12 1/4   ISBN 0-88734-641-3

Available at Bookstores or direct from:

PLAYERS PRESS, Inc.
P.O. Box 1132
Studio City, CA 91614-0132 U.S.A.